LILLENAS DRAMA

FAMILY CAMP

1947

Interactive Dinner Theatre for Outreach

by

Dave Avanzino & Craig Wilson

lillenas
PUBLISHING COMPANY
Kansas City, MO 64141

This is a royalty play. Permission to perform this work is granted when a Production Pack containing scripts for the cast and director is purchased and the royalty is paid two weeks prior to the performance(s). The performance licensing fee for this play is [$35.00] for the first performance and [$25.00] for each subsequent performance. Please use the form in the back of this book to register your performance(s) and to submit the royalty payment. You may make copies of the form or submit the information in the form of a letter.

The following should appear in your printed program:
"Produced by special arrangement with Lillenas Publishing Company."

Lillenas Publishing Company
P. O. Box 419527
Kansas City, MO 64141
Phone: 816-931-1900 * Fax: 816-412-8390
Email: drama@lillenas.com
Web: www.lillenasdrama.com
Printed in the United States

PLEASE NOTE: Songs that are suggested for use in this script are only suggestions. It is the responsibility of the performer(s) to obtain any permission necessary to use such songs. Lillenas Publishing Company is not responsible for any fees when such permission is obtained, nor any damages if permission is not obtained and songs are used illegally.

Cover art by Kevin Williamson
Family Camp logo by Dave Avanzino
Executive Editor: Kim Messer
Copy Editor: Kimberly Meiste
Manuscript Formatting: Karen Phillips
Interior Design by Tom Shank

Dedication

To the God of all creation who shares His creativity with us and gives us the unique ability to create art, music, and theatre to His glory.

We'd also like to dedicate this play to the many people and groups around the country who took a chance on *Uncle Phil's Diner* and used it to glorify God and bless other people. Thank you all for your courage in trying something new. You have no idea what a blessing it has been to us to hear about your success.

Contents

Acknowledgments

We would like to sincerely thank our amazing cast from Community Christian Church in Anaheim Hills, California, for their amazing work and contributions to the creation of this show. We were blessed with a great group of people who jumped into this with both feet and really did an amazing job. Whenever we stage one of these productions for the first time, we are really dependent on the cast to bring it to life and to help us see what works and what doesn't. This talented group of actors really helped us shape the show into the form it is in today and we are very grateful for their help.

We are, once again, grateful to Lillenas Publishing Company for their commitment to us and their support of our work. We're excited about this new show and we are thankful for their trust in us and their willingness to publish it. We hope this addition to their catalog will be a blessing to many people around the country.

We hope that you will enjoy *Family Camp* as much as you have enjoyed the other plays we have been a part of. We love the 1940s and the warm, nostalgic environment that goes along with it. We hope that you and your group will enjoy this production and that it will be a great tool for you to reach your community.

Dave Avanzino and Craig Wilson

Production Notes

An Evening of Interactive Theatre, Food, and Music

The goal behind *Family Camp* is to create a warm, fun, and welcoming environment that the members of your church or group will feel comfortable inviting their friends and family to. It is an unusual collection of improv, music, audience participation, sketch comedy, and food. While there is a definite stage area, the hope is that this event happens all around the guests, including them as often as possible, making them feel a part of it and not just an observer. You are creating an entire environment of sight and sound that includes the entire room. A visit to *Family Camp* is not a passive experience.

While there are specific, scripted events throughout the evening, much of the entertainment comes from the camp staff interacting and improvising with the guests. They often recognize people at the tables since, according to the script, they have all been together at the camp for a week. The script also implies that many of these people have come there for years, so there is a chance to even discuss past events with them. The members of the camp staff might recognize someone from one of their activities like a hike or canoe race and engage them in conversation about it. They interact with one another in small skits and bits designed to amuse people and, at times, include them.

Food and drinks are served to the guests in a buffet style chow line typical of camps. This isn't always necessary but makes for a real camp feel. The menu can be simple and can either be cooked by your own people or catered from outside. Dessert is also served and this can be simple also like slices of pie or cake. Each actor from the cast is assigned certain tables that they will be responsible for interacting with. Even though they are not waiting on those tables and serving them food, they need to make sure that they interact with them during the breaks and give them their own individual show. The evening is designed to run for approximately 2 to 2 and a half hours. Most of the food should be served in the first hour and after that, more of the audiences' attention should be directed up front.

As designed, there is only a short and simple message in the production. The goal is to make people feel welcome and show them how we express our love for God through our creativity and hospitality. This is specifically an outreach event and church members should be encouraged to invite other people. An important goal would be to make the rest of your congregation feel like they have a role in this event just like the actors. Ask them to bring a guest to the performance or participate in the setup and staging of it.

This should be more than just an evening of entertainment for the congregation or group and should be approached as a bridge-building event with the community. You can include some simple information about your church on the tables as well as have information/mailing list cards for people to fill out on the tables. You can also hand them a card as they exit, thanking them for visiting and inviting them back.

Family Camp Outline

The setting of this event is a café-torium at a mountain camp in 1947. Lots of wood paneling line the simple set and various camp items like skis, sleds, animal heads, antlers, etc., can be used as decor. Big Band music plays in the background to create a nostalgic mood. The guests are part of the annual "Family Camp" that has come year after year to this facility. Some who came as children have come so long that they are now bringing their children. The last night of camp is a celebration featuring the annual talent show, games, and camp awards. It is at this event that they hear for the first time that the camp has been sold and how much it is going to change.

Camp Awannahikealotta (A-wanna-hike-a-lot-a) has been in existence for 50 years and has been under the direction of Mr. and Mrs. Bob & Phoebe Dinsdale for 42 of those years. They are a kind, older couple that has made it their life's work to make this camp a blessing for the children and families who have come there year after year. Sadly, the camp has been losing money and the owner has decided to sell it.

Mr. Franklin Abbott and his company CampCo, Inc. have purchased the camp. Mr. Abbott likes camping but he thinks the wave of the future will be to modernize it. In his words, "to bring the great outdoors—indoors!" In his plan there will be no more outdoor campfires. Instead, the amphitheatre will be enclosed and have a nice gas log fire pit. This will mean no more mosquitoes and poison oak to worry about when you don't have any reason to go outside. The new buildings will cover everything but they will have numerous windows you can look out of as well as paintings of what the outside looks like. He is trying to sell his concept to this loyal group of campers and camp staff to convince them to return the following year. At different points in the show he will bring a cast member, like Cookie, up to the stage and tell them about all of the "improvements" he's planning for their particular area of the camp in the hopes of getting their approval. No one likes what he is proposing and they go away dissatisfied with his plans.

During the evening's festivities, dinner and dessert (or just dessert) is served to the guests in a chow line. While the guests are eating their meals, the main cast members (Cast A) will wander through the room and engage each table in conversation. They might help them finish up an incomplete craft project or help them track down their lost and found items. The goal is for each table to be included in this time of interaction with the cast. The kitchen crew (Cast B) can also participate if they are able, but the bulk of this activity is completed by the members of Cast A.

Throughout the evening the guests are included in a variety of games and skits and even a melodrama. Tables will be identified by cabin number and each may be called on during the evening to compete with another cabin to determine the winner of an unfinished event from the previous week, like bird calling. During the melodrama, several guests will be called to the stage to participate and act out the scene for the rest of the audience. Some guests will be featured in the camp awards where their face will be digitally pasted into an existing slide that highlights their accomplishment.

The Annual Staff Talent Show is the highlight of this closing night event. There will be three acts spaced throughout the evening. One song will be lip-synced to an Andrews Sisters-like number. It was originally suppose to be three women, but one is ill so they draft Biff Martin to fill the third spot. Biff is uncomfortable but eventually gets into it. Another selection is a staff Kazoo song, and the final number was supposed to be a ballet, but Andy pleads to have the spot so he can recite a love poem to Penny to win her back.

Near the end of the show, the staff begins to think back on their years at the camp and each one picks up something off the stage, telling a small story about it and why it's meaningful to them. The Dinsdales let each staff member keep the memento. Stuart picks up the deer head and tells the story about the time his dad was driving him up to camp and hit the deer with his car. Mr. Abbott becomes so moved by all of these testimonies (as well as the rest of the evening's events) that he finally decides to keep the camp the same and not change anything—providing the Dinsdales agree to continue to manage it. He asks the crowd if they want them back and they cheer. The Dinsdales agree to come back as do the rest of the staff.

Cast

It is recommended that you have 2 types of casts in this production: Cast A and Cast B:

1) Cast A members are the main driving force of the show and have the most lines to memorize and further the story line of the show throughout the evening. They are also mainly responsible for interacting with the guests at their tables. They range in age from high school to senior citizens. Some of the ages of the characters can be modified to fit your available cast members. This type of interactive theatre event requires a lot from your Cast A actors. They need to be able to improvise, stay in character, act, and be prepared for anything that might come up. You need to be able to trust them to know what is funny, as well as what is not funny, as you let them loose in the room. If you have really talented high schooler's that can handle the amount of improv and confidence necessary, go for it. The roles played by older characters are best played by people of the approximate age as opposed to trying to age someone in their 20s to play a 70 year-old. Cast A characters will be "onstage" for the entire evening. This cast is designed to provide much of the entertainment on and off stage during this evening. They are what people will remember the most, so they need to be able to improvise well with the guests.

2) Cast B (the Kitchen Crew) is another group of characters, in costume, that are there mainly to clear the tables and keep drinks refilled. They are described as high school students trying to win a scholarship to camp next year by having a competition to win votes from the people at their tables. There are four groups: Science Camp, Music Camp, Sports Camp, and Bonnie Belle Camp. Each of these groups needs at least one person in it that will have some lines and be the representative onstage when called. The speaking parts can be split among a couple of different people if desired. This group has a much lower commitment level and can even be different from night to night. They need to be in costume but don't need to learn all of the things the other cast members do. You can use your high school group or different Bible or Sunday School classes each night. You can decide how many you need based on how many tables you plan to have at your event. The members of this group with speaking roles do need to attend some of the Cast A rehearsals in order to be worked into the stage scenes.

Rehearsing

This is a difficult piece to rehearse since many of the elements require a live audience to play off of. It is not always necessary to have everyone at every rehearsal. What is suggested is that you rehearse the Cast A members as much as necessary to get the scripted parts of the show memorized and blocked. You can then work with them on what they will say to the guests at their tables as well as work up bits of business with one another that can be performed table-side for the guests. For example, Biff can talk with each cast member about what they need to do before the camp closes down for the season. You can bring the speaking members of Cast B into some of the rehearsals to plug them in and get them familiar with where their parts come into the show.

As you get closer to the event, bring in all of Cast B and walk through the show with them so they too are familiar with it and know what parts they need to participate in. You can set up a room with chairs to represent the amount of tables you will have the night of your event. Assign cast members their tables and begin practicing moving around in character and interacting with each other. If possible, bring in some people for the dress rehearsal to act as guests that can be used in the audience participation sections, and also to give the cast someone to interact with. Be sure to rehearse ALL of the audience participation pieces with people including the Bird Call Contest and the Melodrama. Your cast needs to see how these work with actual people to figure how best to perform them.

The goal is for the cast to become familiar with the series of events for the evening. You will never know exactly what it will be like until you get guests in the room, so the more familiar everyone is with the order of the show, the easier it will go. It is recommended that you bring in all of your Cast B for your final dress rehearsal (and possibly sooner) so they will also have some idea of what to expect. Your rehearsals will generally be much shorter than the actual performances so don't worry. It can be helpful to print up a small list of events (a cheat sheet) for cast members to carry around with them. This can be a helpful reminder of what scene you are on and what event is coming up next.

• **NOTE on appropriate improvisation.** The main reason for getting together and practicing the cast improvs together is to determine if there are certain things that might be inappropriate to use. A lot of things that might seem funny can be insulting or offensive to people. Putting down each other or making fun of each other can be funny but can also be viewed as mean. Just be aware of what you are saying and remember who your audience is. You also need to remember that this event is set in 1947 so contemporary slang words and phrases, as well as references, need to be edited out of your improvs. You can find great resources online for 30s and 40s fads, slang, pop culture, and more. The more your cast knows of the era, the more they can bring people into the environment.

Food Service and Suggestions

Since you are trying to recreate a mountain camp environment, you can have a simple menu of 1 or 2 main entrees, salad, and a side dish or two. A sample menu would be chicken and some kind of beef (ribs, pot roast, etc.), potatoes (mashed, scalloped, etc.) a vegetable, and salad. These can be set out in a buffet style setting, which is what you would typically have at a camp. There will always be someone who doesn't like what you serve but you can't help that. If you feel like you need to have a vegetarian option, it is good to prepare for that in advance. Remember that the food is only one element of the evening. Hopefully the entire evening will be so memorable that any shortcomings in the food will be forgotten. Obviously, you can get more elaborate if your budget and facilities allow.

One way to involve more people from your congregation is to line up a Bible school class or other ministry group to handle all of the food preparation. This takes a great burden off of the cast and makes it more of a church-wide event. If you prefer, you can use the cast to serve the food to people at their tables in more of a restaurant-style instead of the buffet line, but the buffet line is more typical of a camp setup and is easier to execute.

Another suggestion is to have someone come in and cater the event. Shop around and see what kind of deal you can get. Handing this element over to an outside source may be worth it compared to doing it yourselves.

Cookie needs to be part of the food service line since he/she is, technically, the camp cook. Put Cookie around the table helping serve food to the guests and other cast members can help with this as well. This is a good opportunity to interact with the guests and improv. Since the cabin is in the woods, you can have some fun with the guests by telling them that you're serving squirrel and raccoon which Cookie trapped herself. You do need to be careful if you do this that you don't scare some people (especially kids) away from the food. There is a fine line between joking with them and grossing them out.

It is best to get the main food out of the way early and then focus more on the entertainment. As guests are seated, Cast B takes their drink orders. After Scene 1, guests are excused by table (Biff or another cast member can do this) to get in the chow line. Getting the meal out of the way as soon as possible is preferable because, while people are eating, it is hard for them to focus their attention away from the table. This is the most time that Cast A spends interacting with the guests and each other throughout the room. Later in the evening, the cast members can serve dessert to guests at their table. It is advisable to have enough drinks to be able to gives refills throughout the evening. This gives your cast members a good reason to continue to visit their tables.

You can use round or rectangular tables but you will need to leave space enough for people to walk through. Don't overcrowd the room for the sake of getting more people in. It will make the type of entertainment going on more difficult.

If you decide a full meal is too much trouble or expense, just do a dessert. You can serve ice cream sundaes, banana splits, Oreos, chocolate shakes, pie, etc. You will need to determine where in the evening you wish to do this and adjust the lines in the script to accommodate it. If you are only serving dessert, wait a little while before doing so. You can start off with serving coffee and drinks and bring out the food later in the evening.

•**NOTE:** Scene 1 can be long so everyone needs to keep it moving so that you can get to the meal as soon as possible. If you feel the need to get to it faster, here is a suggestion. After Cookie does his/her intro, Bob comments on her "Breakfast-on-a-stick" and then asks her if dinner is almost ready, and she says it will be in a few more minutes. Bob continues to introduce Nurse Brickman and then she has her conversation with Biff about his recent wound. After that Cookie pops back in and says dinner is ready. Bob invites the Chaplain up to pray and then the tables are released for dinner. After everyone has their food, Bob comes back up and introduces the kitchen crew and the scholarship competition. When this is concluded, everyone is then free to finish the meal. When it is determined that the meal is finished, Biff returns to stage and picks up the staff intros with Andy. After Lester (the final introduction), Bob cuts to the end of Scene 1 and reminds everyone of what the evening has in store, telling them they will be right back. This leads to the Scene 1 Break.

This format gets to the meal faster and works better if you have a start time of 7 P.M. or later. If you start at 6 P.M. or earlier the original format will work. The motivation behind this is if you start later then your guests will be hungrier and, since they know that food is coming, they will get impatient if Scene 1 goes on too long. One suggestion is to have some bread or crackers already on the table to give them something to snack on while they wait.

Ticket Sales

If it is possible to do this event without charging, go for it. This will make a great impression on your guests. For most of us, this is not possible. This is just a suggestion but if you need to charge, sell tickets as opposed to having an offering. Visitors expect an offering and one of the goals of events like these is to show them the unexpected. In selling tickets, target your congregation to purchase them for their guests. Explain your goals and your needs, and get them on board with your vision of outreach to the community. If they can understand that this is their role to play in this event, they will more than likely get excited about it with you. You can also sell the guest tickets for ½ the price of the member tickets. This helps cover your costs and helps them to become a part of it with you.

You can either sell tickets with assigned seating or general admission. Selling assigned seats can speed up the actual seating of guests, but it does take more time and effort to organize. Try to sell as many "pre-sale" tickets as possible. You will always have walk-ins but it is easier if you know exactly how many people to plan for, especially when food is involved. Offer an incentive for people to plan ahead by charging more at the door for tickets than you do pre-sale tickets. You may want to set aside a certain number of tickets for each night specifically for walk-ins. It can leave a bad impression if people get turned away at the door, especially visitors.

Seating

The goal is to get people seated as fast as possible. The evening's events can start as soon as the first person walks in the door. Wait until you have a large group of people waiting to come in before you begin seating. Have a couple of people taking tickets and then have Bob and Phoebe Dinsdale welcoming guests as they enter the main room or at the front door. The other cast members can help guests find a table, which are labeled by Cabin Number and a woodland animal. If you'd like, you can have someone assigning tables from a floor plan. The tables need to have numbers and as she gives the guests a table number, a cast member can take them to their seats and she can cross out those seats on her floor plan. Or you can simply take their tickets and let them find their own seating.

The atmosphere of the event needs to begin from the moment they are in line waiting to come in. You can have cast members walking around outside talking with them or talking to each other in front of them. To create a woodsy environment, have as many people as possible bring their artificial Christmas trees and set them up outside your building's front door. You can also make a wood sign with the camp logo on it. The more you can do to create the atmosphere and environment from the start, the better. Make sure there is Big Band music playing in the background as soon as guests walk in.

A couple of suggestions regarding room set up. First of all, don't over pack your tables. You will need adequate room for the cast members to move easily through the room for food service and several of the evening's events. You also want your guests to feel comfortable and squeezing too many people in won't help accomplish this. There are also issues of safety and fire codes to be considered. Another thing to consider is the placement of your stage area. If you have a long room with a stage at one end, you might consider putting the stage area along the long wall instead of at the end. This makes it easier to see from most of the tables and keeping it at more of an audience level, instead of up on a stage, makes your guests feel more a part of it. (See Suggested Room Layout on page 19.)

Costuming

Costuming for *Family Camp* is relatively easy. However, remember you are trying to re-create 1947 as much as possible. A lot of the personalities for the Cast A characters are expressed through their clothing, so it is recommended that you don't have everyone in some kind of camp uniform. You might consider having T-shirts made with the Camp Awannahikealotta logo on it that cast members can wear along with other costume pieces.

A tan or khaki shirt can be that unifying costume element that identifies the cast as camp workers. Characters like Biff, Stuart, and Lester are career camp workers and would have the strongest "camper" look with canteens, belts, hats, ropes, khaki shorts or

Suggested Room Layout

Stage is centered along side wall of room rather than at one end. This allows the audience to be more a part of the action rather than removed from it. Keeping the stage low (2'-3') helps this also.

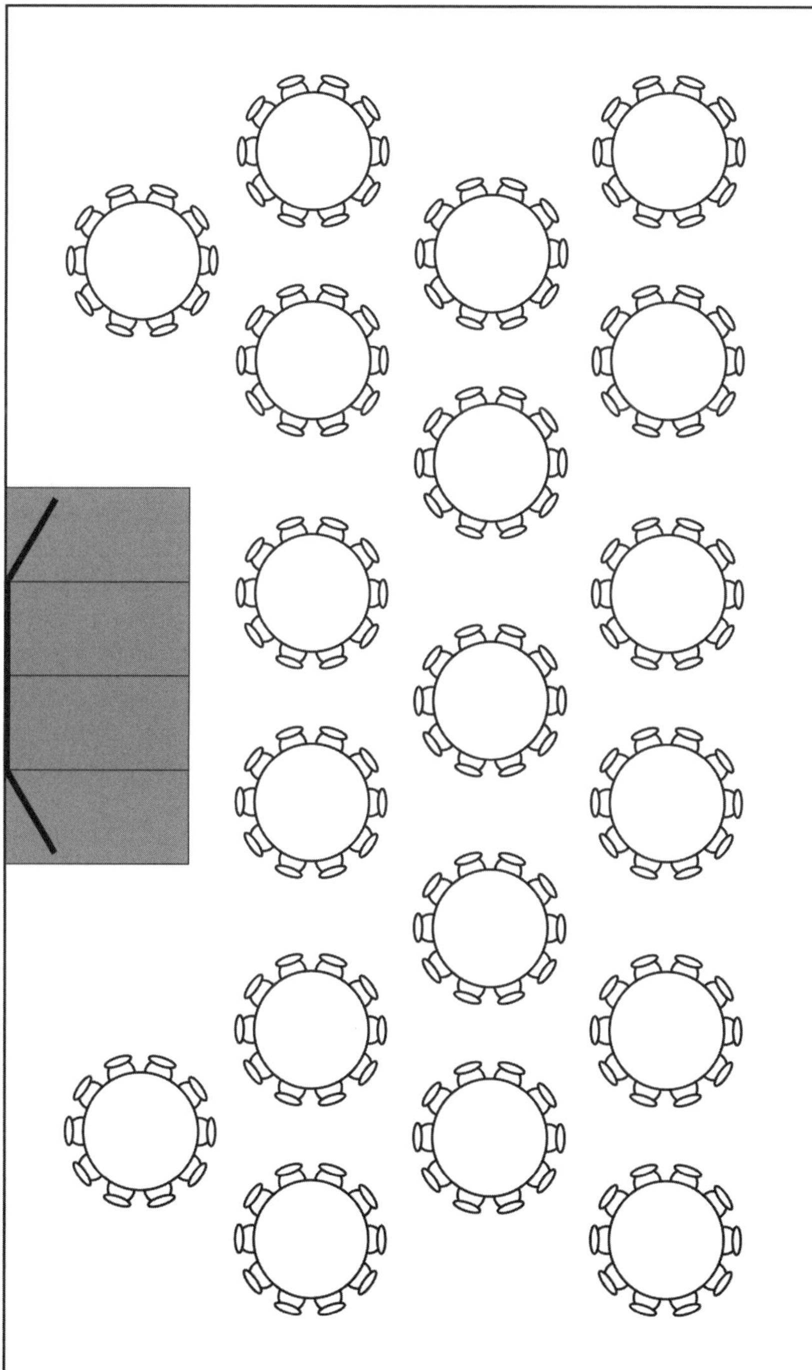

pants, etc. The other cast members, like Andy and Susie, might wear the shirt and a pair of jeans with some kind of hat, bandana or other accessory. Penny is a camp guest, not a camp worker, and would wear some kind of period dress or a more casual outfit with jeans. Nurse Brickman wears a dress or pants and a white nurse jacket and hat. Cookie can wear the camp T-shirt with a dirty apron over it.

The Dinsdales are dressed nicely for the evening. She could wear a dress and he could wear slacks, a button shirt, and cardigan sweater. There are plenty of books and internet resources on the 40s that you can find for period costume suggestions. You can also rent movies set in the 40s for costume ideas. Hair can also help define the era so be sure to look for references on this also. A suggestion for your Cast B members is to print the camp logo on different color T-shirts for each camp group. This will help the audience identify which group they are from. They can wear pants or skirts with them and accentuate them for their particular group.

See online reference photos "Family Camp Cast", "Costume-Khaki T-shirt" and "Costume-Color T-shirt" for additional costuming ideas. Resources online can be downloaded by going to www.lillenasdrama.com and searching for the *Family Camp* product page. Once there, find the section titled "Sample Pages" to find all resources.

For *Family Camp* products including T-shirts for the cast, mugs, and other logo products, you can contact: familycamp@totce.com. A list of available products and pricing will be sent to you. You can also look us up online at www.totce.com, or call 800.520.0025.

Technical

This production requires a lot of continuous recorded music as well as sound effects and roving actors. You will need to determine what will work best for you in setting this up. If you have access to wireless lapel or headset mics you can use them as needed for some of the actors. The general camp staff typically doesn't need wireless microphones. Their improv out in the room only needs to be heard by their immediate tables. If it needs to be louder, they can yell. Since most of what happens onstage is in the context of announcements, most of the actors can stand and speak into a microphone on a stand. Since it is supposed to be 1947 make sure they are corded microphones on stands, not a wireless handheld mic. You may even be able to find some period microphones or make something. Some of the characters, like Cookie, might be entering and exiting from the back of the room for their lines and would need a wireless lapel mic to be heard. As you rehearse you will figure out if other actors need them and when.

Recorded Big Band music should be playing whenever the action onstage takes a break. This keeps the environment going when the actors stop speaking. There are other sound effects throughout the evening that can be played from recorded files by the sound technician. Lillenas has three Sound Effects CDs that may provide some of what you need as well as individual on-line downloadable sounds. Check them out at: www.lillenasdrama.com

•**NOTE:** To locate free music in the public domain you can check out the following site: http://www.archive.org. There is a music section where you can find public domain Big Band music for use as background music. Not everything on this site is public domain so be sure to check before using.

Lighting

There is very little specialty lighting for this production. You will need overall, preferably dimmable, room lighting for your guests to see what they are eating and some focused lighting on your stage area. As the evening goes along, it may get harder and harder to get everyone's attention to the stage. You can always dim the room lighting and boost the stage lighting at certain points to get their attention focused where you want it.

Video Projection

If you choose to do the Camp Awards presentation you will need to be able to project the digital slides onto a screen. You can also project the "Camp Motto" slide for the audience to recite in Scene 1.

Creative Leadership Team

As with any type of production, the more organized you are and the more people you can get involved the better. This event is designed to be an outreach to your community and is best accomplished if it becomes more of a church-wide project rather than just a music or drama department project. There are many areas that a variety of people can get involved in and take charge of outside of the performance areas. This gives a great opportunity for different members of your church to partner together in this outreach.

The main positions you need to think about are the following*:

- PRODUCER
- DIRECTOR
- MUSICAL DIRECTOR
- SETS AND ROOM DECOR
- TECHNICAL DIRECTOR
- FOOD PRODUCTION COORDINATOR
- MINISTRY COORDINATOR
- ADVERTISING COORDINATOR

PRODUCER: The producer is responsible for making sure everyone else gets their job done and tries to make the event run smoothly and pleasantly for all involved. He/She oversees all the elements of the production (i.e., room reservation, food preparation, rehearsal schedules, and personnel involvement). This requires a detail-oriented person who is a good motivator and encourager.

DIRECTOR: The director is mainly responsible for the cast and the shape and direction the show will take. He/She may be directly involved in other areas like the set, lighting, etc. During the show, it is recommended that the director be "onstage" in costume (not necessarily responsible for interacting with the guests) to keep the show moving along. He or she can move through the room and communicate with both actors and the sound techs to cue each new event. This is needed to keep the evening moving along at a good pace. The director can actually be a member of the cast if needed.

* Some of these positions can be combined.

•**NOTE:** During the actual production, the director is the one who decides the length of the breaks between scenes. Once the meal is done, he/she can decide to make the breaks shorter and shorter to keep the show moving along. After dessert is served, the breaks can be as short as a minute or two.

MUSICAL DIRECTOR: This person is needed only if you require help in performing *Yankee Doodle Dandy* on kazoos. This song can be very simple and corny or it can be more elaborate with parts, harmonies, etc., which would require the help of a musical director to arrange and rehearse it.

TECHNICAL DIRECTOR/LIGHTS AND SOUND: Responsible for arranging all technical elements for the evening including lighting, sound system, and video. Also needs to arrange for a crew to run lights and sound.

SETS AND ROOM DÉCOR: Responsible for designing and building sets for the evening as well as dressing the room, entryway, and table tops. Also responsible for overseeing the striking of the set when done.

FOOD PRODUCTION: Responsible for providing for all of the food to be served. If the food is being catered, they need to work with the caterer on menu, budget, scheduling, setup, etc., to insure that everything is prepared in time for the event. If the food is going to be prepared by people from the group, they will need to work with them on menu, budget, and scheduling to make sure that they have everything they need to get the job done on time. This could be taken over by a Bible school class, men's or women's group, etc.

MINISTRY COORDINATOR: Responsible for all of the personnel working the event other than the cast members. This is the person who works to recruit setup and tear-down crews, clean up, kitchen help, food preparation, etc. One suggestion is to get different Bible school classes to volunteer to adopt a night to work the event or adopt a night where they will commit to bringing a guest. This person is also responsible for getting out the message of outreach to your group through announcements, etc.

ADVERTISING: This is important if you hope to get visitors. The best way to get them, however, is if your members invite them. Work on ways to advertise "why" you are doing this event to your church and get them onboard with your vision. You can print up a 40s style invitation they can hand out to their friends. Many local papers and radio stations have free listings for events like these that you may be able to take advantage of also.

Set Design and Decor

This production requires little or even no set to work. You can simply decorate the existing walls of your room or you can build a small set consisting of a few flats (see Set Options 1 & 2 on pages 26 & 27). It is best to get the stage area off of the floor a little—about 2-3 feet is best. Your guests will be sitting, but by raising the stage a little you will improve the sight lines and make the action onstage more visible. If the stage gets too high, the audience may feel more removed from the action and less a part of it.

If you build flats, one idea is to incorporate a swinging door that would lead offstage into the "kitchen". This is how characters, mostly Cookie, can enter the stage from the "kitchen". The staging does not require a door, so it is not necessary. If everyone just enters from the side of the stage it will be fine also. Cookie can come from the back of the room and reference the kitchen as being somewhere else.

The room is supposed to be a café-torium at a camp in 1947, so you can create simple flats with wood paneling to achieve this look. A fireplace in the middle with brick can add some interest. (Faux brick paneling is available at home improvement warehouses.) If you use video projection you can build the set around the screen or just have one off to the side. Most of the set decor pieces on the stage are specific to the plot in Scene 6. Some of the framed photos are available at www.lillenasdrama.com for downloading or you can find other images yourself. See the prop list for a more detailed description. In addition to these elements, you can add other cabin/camping elements like antique skis, fishing poles, antlers, pictures, etc. Thrift stores are a good place to get a lot of these kinds of set decor. Make sure that there isn't anything that is too contemporary for 1947. You can find great period artwork in calendars and then frame the images. Images from Currier and Ives, the Audubon Society, and even some of Norman Rockwell's images all fit the period decor.

• See online reference photo "Family Camp Set" for additional scenery ideas.

• There are additional set designs available online for download if needed.

For the tables, simple tablecloths and placemats dress them up. In the center, you create some sort of tacky centerpiece with pinecones, which is mentioned in the script. If you have a cup in the center of the arrangement you can put all of the silverware or plastic ware in it. If you are going to seat people by table numbers you will need to have some identification on the tables. Small signs on sticks attached to the centerpieces can accomplish this. Remember that this is supposed to be 1947, not just look like it.

• See online reference photo "Centerpiece Ideas" for additional centerpiece ideas.

• The artwork files for the centerpiece cabin numbers are titled, "Cabin Numbers 1-4, 5-8 & 9-12". They can be downloaded, printed onto card stock, cut, and then glued together onto a wood skewer and attached to the centerpieces.

The poster artwork that is downloadable online can be enlarged at many copying stores or blueprint businesses. Some 18 x 24 copiers will even take your own paper. You can buy colored art papers at an art store and then enlarge the designs onto them. These can then be painted or colored to add more impact. Blueprint copiers can go up to 4' wide by any length but usually only onto white paper. You can also find a lot of historical forestry and travel posters online that can be downloaded and enlarged for use as wall decor.

There are two different logos available for download at www.lillenasdrama.com. The file called, "FC Logo" is for use on advertising, tickets, etc. It is the logo for the production called, "Family Camp." The other logo file, called, "A Camp Logo" is the camp logo for "Camp Awannahikealotta." This logo can be used on T-shirts, posters or other decor used in the room. It is not intended for advertising since it refers to the camp location and not the name of the show itself.

There are lots of resources on the internet for finding old photographs of camp life. By searching for images with terms like "historical, camp, photos" you can find numerous sites with great images. These can be downloaded, printed, framed, and hung on your set or around the room to add to your decor.

SET OPTION WITH VIDEO SCREEN

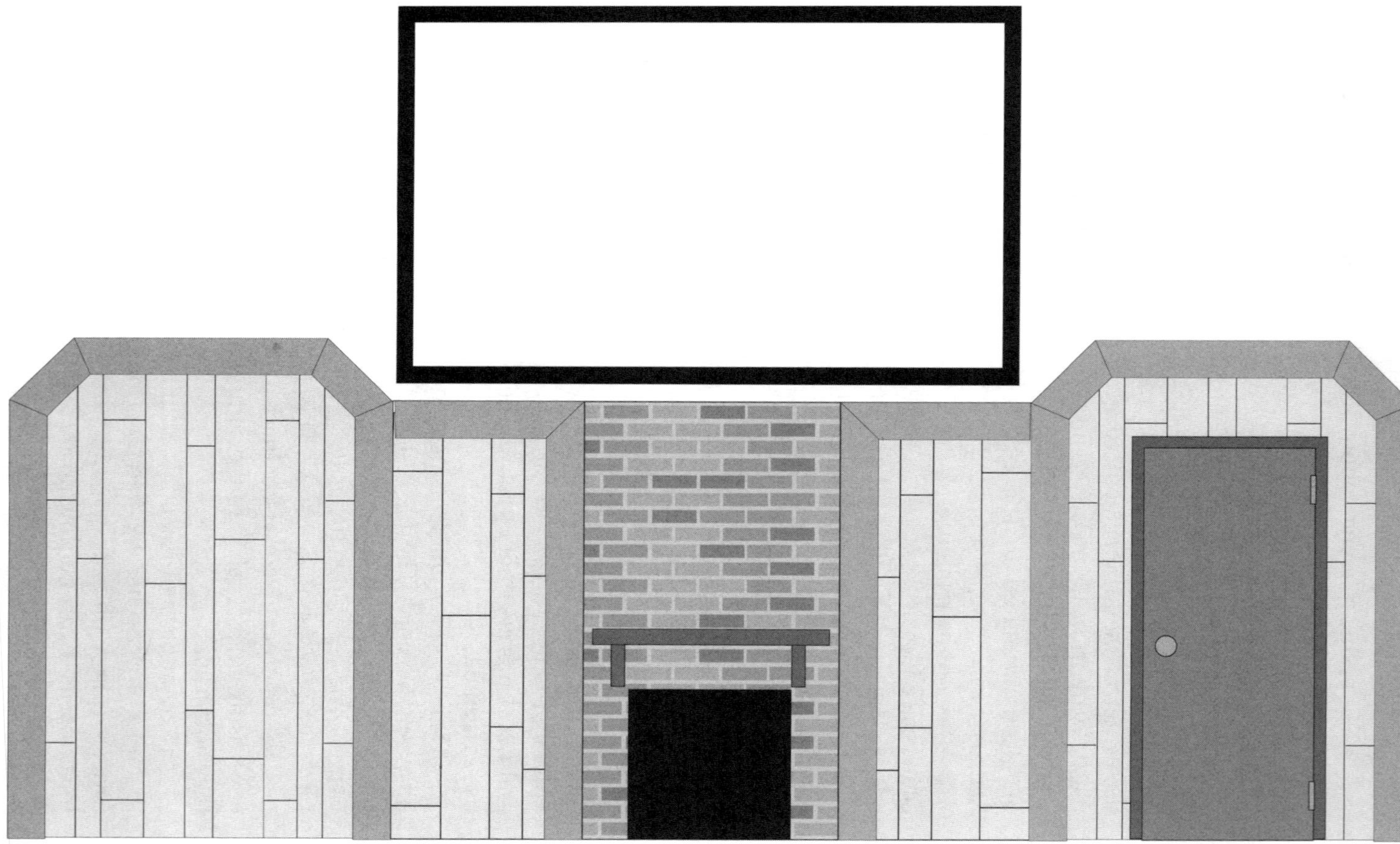

Optional Door

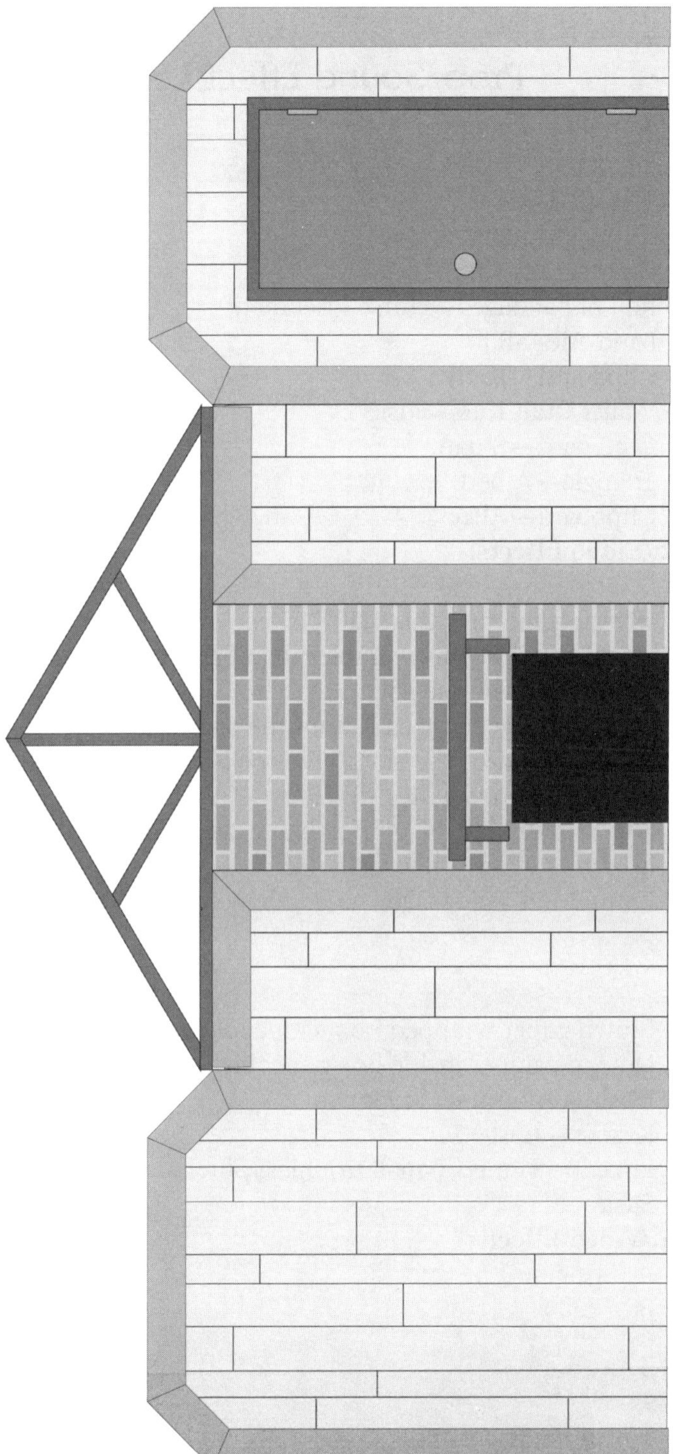

SET OPTION WITH FRAME STRUCTURE

Optional Door

Prop/Sound Effect List

Scene 1

Props:

- Whistle—Biff
- Clipboard—Biff
- Dirty socks—Biff
- Roll of bandages—Nurse Brickman
- Band-Aid—Biff
- Clipboard—Andy
- Wallet Craft Kits—Susie
- Clipboard—Stuart
- Triangle—Albert
- Clipboard—Alice

Sound/Video Effects:

- Bell ringing—This can be a recorded effect or you can actually ring the bell that will be seen in Scene 6. Ringing the actual bell is actually simpler than using a recorded sound. It can be done by the sound tech from the booth each time. In Scene 5, Phoebe takes it from the sound tech after it is rung and carries it to the stage. Two bell/chime sound effects can be found on *Sound Effects for Church Productions, Vol. 1* [7-65762-05422-6] or purchased as individual MP3 downloadables at www.lillenasdrama.com).
- Camp Motto slide (Download file name: "Motto Slide")

Scene 2

Props:

- Brown paper wrapped box with cookie crumbs—Biff
- Note to camper inside box of cookies—Biff
- Flashlight—Nurse Brickman
- Kazoos—Cast
- Prize for winners (small trophies, purchased or handmade)—Susie

Sound/Video Effects:

- Bell ringing
- Bird calls

Scene 3

Props:

- Finger bandage—Biff

- Thick glasses—Biff
- Costume elements for trio

Sound/Video Effects:

- Bell ringing
- Recorded song for lip-sync

Scene 4

Props:

- Bandage—Biff
- Clipboard—Alice
- Melodrama signs, "Boo" and "Yeah"
- Costume elements for melodrama characters
- "Deed"—Rolled up paper
- Plunger

Sound/Video Effects:

- Bell ringing
- Slides for Camp Awards

Scene 5

Props:

- Arm sling—Biff
- Frozen underwear (cardboard glued to inside of boxer shorts. Spray on some splotches with white paint and add glitter)—Stuart
- Camp bell—Phoebe
- Aerosol can with water (can add "Pine in a Can" label)—Abbott
- Satchel—Stuart
- Mr. Nutters puppet (Suggestion: Grey Squirrel Puppet from Folkmanis Puppets)—Stuart

Sound/Video Effects:

- Bell ringing
- Sappy music behind poem—Use a song like *Peer Gynt Suite No. 1, Opus 46:1. Morning Mood*
- Nature sounds

Scene 6

Props:

- Camp bell—Biff

- Photo of old campers (on set). Photo image "Campers" from the website. No glass in frame. You can also find your own image if preferred.
- Photo of baptism (on set). Photo image "Baptism" from the website. No glass in frame. You can also find your own image if preferred.
- Flag (on set). This can be a flag on a pole in a stand or a folded up flag.
- Landscape painting (on set). This should be an actual painting as opposed to a print or poster. Borrow one or look in thrift stores.
- Rough wooden cross (on set). This is made from 2 pieces of wood. Should look a little burned.
- Plaque (on set). Photo image "Plaque" from the website. Mount to a wood plaque.
- Deer head (on set). Borrow one if possible.
- Burnt toast. Can be real or created from ½" foam core.
- Spray smoke. Can use a small fogger for this.
- Color cards on tables. These are made to match the color of the Kitchen Crew T-shirts. (Download file name: "Color Cards")
- Bear badge patch. Need to have tape on the back so it can be placed on Lester by Mr. Dinsdale.

Sound/Video Effects:

None

Family Camp Products for Cast and Audience

For *Family Camp* products including T-shirts for the cast, mugs, and other logo products, you can contact: familycamp@totce.com. A list of available products and pricing will be sent to you. You can also look us up online at www.totce.com, or call 800.520.0025

FAMILY CAMP

19 47

Pre-Show

Guests arrive. Big Band music is playing. Guests are seated at tables with cabin numbers and cabin names on them. Cast A and Cast B members greet them and explain their dinner menu and drink choices. Since it's a camp, there will most likely be only one or two entrées available. Cast B members can bring their drinks to the table during this time. The Cast B members will have names and will be from one of four different groups of kids including Music Camp, Science Camp, Sports Camp, and Bonnie Belle Camp. They can have a character name and can interact and improv with guests if they feel comfortable doing that, but the main part of the improv will be handled by Cast A. Cast A members can also be circulating and improving with the guests during this time. At each place there will be a printed place mat for the guests to fill out including puzzles, a maze, "Animal Footprints," and "Camp Word Search." (Place mat artwork is found at www.lillenasdrama.com on the *Family Camp* product page under "Sample Images." Downloadable file name: "Place mat.") The camp photographer will be roaming around the room taking pictures that will be used later in the slide show.

Scene 1

(Lights up on stage area. Bob *and* Phoebe Dinsdale *enter and come to mic.)*

Bob: Welcome everyone to the last night of this years' Family Camp at Camp Awannahikealotta. Phoebe and I hope that you've all had as much fun this week as we've had. We've been running this camp for over 40 years . . .

Phoebe *(sticks her head into the microphone and corrects him):* It's 42 to be exact.

Bob: Right. And it's been so great for us to see so many people who came to this camp as kids are now bringing their own kids.

Phoebe: And even their grandkids.

Bob: Uh-huh. Our little camp has always been a place where people have been able to get away from the city and into the great outdoors where they can meet God in the midst of His creation.

Phoebe: That's right, Bob. Now, I know I say this every year but I think that this year was the best ever. *(Getting choked up)* It's hard to imagine us doing anything else.

Bob: Steady girl. *(To* Phoebe*)* We decided that we wouldn't talk about that until later tonight.

Phoebe: I'm sorry. I know.

Bob: OK. Well, I think the best way to start off this evening is for everyone to recite the camp motto. So let's stand and say it together.

(Slide can be projected with motto. Slide image found at www.lillenasdrama.com on the Family Camp *product page under "Sample Images." Downloadable file name: "Motto Slide")*

Camp Awannahikealotta
Land of valleys, hills, and watta
For moms and dads and sons and daughtas
Come and see us, you just gotta

Bob: That never fails to bring a tear to my eye. Have a seat everyone. There are some last minute announcements that the staff needs to make. So, first of all, we have Cookie the camp chef.

Phoebe: No dear, actually Biff is going first.

BOB: OK. Here's Camp Director Biff Martin

BIFF *(enters and blows whistle to get attention):* All right everyone, listen up. The Biffster has got some important announcements to make. I heard a few of you talking today, and you know who you are, about how many rules there are at camp. When I was in the Marines we had all sorts of rules and I'm a better man today because of those rules. And judging by some of the unsanctioned and unendorsed extracurricular activities many of you have taken part in this week, we obviously need a reminder of the rules even on the very last night of camp.

(PHOEBE *takes the mic.)*

PHOEBE: Now, Biff, you must remember that these people are not soldiers like you were.

BIFF: I know, Mrs. Dinsdale. I'm just trying to keep the peace and install a little order around here. For instance, let's talk about camp pranks. The camp bell has been missing since the second day of camp. While I understand the classic nature and history of stealing the camp bell every year as a prank, I don't appreciate it nor do I think it's funny. *(He addresses an audience member.)* You, sir, in the back. I heard you snickering. Do you know something about the bell? No? Well, in case you do, I wanted to let you know that if someone turns it in, I'm offering complete and total amnesty—with a catch. You'll just have latrine duty tomorrow morning at 0400.

A couple of other items of importance. There are a few of you who still owe money to the snack shack. We'll be holding your luggage as collateral until you clear that up so you better take care of it by tomorrow. Finally, we have a lot of lost and found items we'll be bringing out through the night for you to claim and take home. Our first item is this pair of dirty socks that desperately need to find their owner. (BIFF *holds up a dirty pair of socks.)* Anyone? Oh, I see a hand over here. (BIFF *points to a guest, walks over and hands them the socks.)* Here you go. Can you please take these as far away from the food as possible? Thanks. All right, remember campers, rules are safety, and "Safety is no accident." *(Bell rings in the distance)* That was the camp bell. I'd know that sound anywhere. I'm coming for you! *(Runs out)*

(COOKIE *enters from the kitchen door and takes the mic.)*

COOKIE: I have a brief announcement about tomorrow's breakfast. Since the buses are leaving early there won't be time to come into the hall for breakfast, so I'll be serving my famous "Breakfast on a Stick." What I do is fry an egg, put some bacon on it, wrap it in a pancake, dip it in syrup, put it on a stick, and deep fry it. We give it to you with about 20 napkins so you can eat it on the bus. They'll be ready early so come by and grab one in the morning on your way out.

BOB *(disgusted):* Thanks, Cookie. I think I'll wait until we get down the mountain to have some breakfast, but that sounds delicious. I think that Nurse Brickman has some final things to wrap up. Is she here? Nurse Brickman? We're ready for you.

NURSE BRICKMAN *(comes to stage trailing a long roll of ace bandages that are attached at the other end to a guest's arm):* I'm coming, I'm coming! I was just finishing up a demo for Cabin 7 on the proper way to wrap a sprained wrist. Don't worry, sir. I'll finish up in just a minute. In the meantime, keep that arm elevated. *(She keeps reminding the guest to keep his arm up if he drops it down.)* I have just one announcement to make. We are running extremely low on calamine lotion due to the ill-fated, unguided nature hike some of the young people took. Anyway, not to worry, Cookie has whipped up a batch of her home remedy anti-itch cream made from oatmeal, clam juice, and garlic. See me if you need some. If you can't find me, just follow the smell.

BIFF *(returns with a Band-Aid on his forehead):* Hear that, campers? Poison Ivy! One more reason to follow the rules. Rules lead to safety, and "Safety is no accident." (NURSE BRICKMAN *repeats the last part of "Safety is no accident" with* BIFF. *It is obvious that she has heard him say this many times.)*

NURSE BRICKMAN *(to* BIFF*):* Biff, what happened to your head?

BIFF *(embarrassed):* I was running to find the camp bell and I ran into a tree.

NURSE BRICKMAN: I can take a look at that for you if you want.

BIFF *(toughing it out):* I'm OK, but thanks. (NURSE BRICKMAN *returns to guest with the bandage.)* All right, who's next? *(Looks at clipboard)* Andy Thompson, our Aquatic Director. Oh, there he is. Come on up, Andy.

ANDY: Hi, everyone. It's been a good camp this year. We only lost 2 canoes, 1 sailboat, and 12 paddles, which is a big improvement from last year, so give yourselves a hand. I'm taking sign-ups tonight for our final "Polar Bear Swim" of the week in the lake tomorrow morning at 5 a.m. Even though I said it will be our final swim of the week, it would actually be our first since no one has shown up to any of the other ones. I'm hopeful though, so I'll be coming around to get your names down. Thanks for another great camp.

PHOEBE *(crosses and keeps* ANDY *from leaving):* Now, Andy. We all know that this week you reconnected with Penny Knight, your camp sweetheart from 20 years ago. Did you think that you were going to get away from here without telling us how things are going with you two?

ANDY *(embarrassed):* Well, Mrs. Dinsdale, I was sure going to try. We've had a great week together, and we're hopeful that things will continue when we get home. We found out that we only live one town apart.

PHOEBE *(excited):* That's great! Well, let's get Penny up here and show you two kids off to the world. Penny! Penny Knight? Where are you girl? Oh, there you are. Come up here and join us. (PENNY *joins them onstage.)* Now, I understand that you two met 20* years ago this week when you were both kids at this Family Camp, is that right? *(*Note: The number of years can change based on the age of the people playing* PENNY *and* ANDY.*)*

PENNY *(shyly):* Yes, ma'am. That's right.

PHOEBE *(unsure):* And I seem to remember that your first meeting involved a canoe and some sort of daring rescue?

PENNY: Yes, it did. A canoe capsized on the lake.

PHOEBE: Well, what could be more romantic? A lovely young girl falls into the lake and a handsome young man rushes down and jumps in to save her. Is that how it happened, Andy?

ANDY *(uncomfortable, nervous):* Well, sort of. That's pretty close to what happened. Yeah. *(He tries to leave.)*

PHOEBE: Well, I'm sure that everyone here would like to hear *exactly* how it happened, right folks? Did you jump in and save her or what?

ANDY *(nervously)*: Well, we were both in the water and it's hard to say who was doing what at the time because there was a lot of splashing and shouting and . . .

PHOEBE *(confused)*: I don't understand what you mean.

PENNY: What he's trying hard *not* to say is that *he* was the one that capsized the canoe, and that *I* was the one who jumped in and saved him.

PHOEBE *(trying to make the best of it)*: Oh! Well! That's a nice story too. And the point is that you met and that you fell in love. That's what matters. And I seem to remember, Andy, that you wrote Penny a lovely poem that next year.

ANDY: Oh, yeah. I'd forgotten about that.

PHOEBE: Do you think that you could recite it for us?

ANDY: Oh no, Mrs. Dinsdale. It's been so long I couldn't possibly remember it now.

PHOEBE: All right. Well you two kids go off and have a nice dinner and we'll get another update later. Biff, who's next on your long list of announcements? Remember, these people need to eat tonight.

BIFF: I know. We're getting through them as fast as we can. If we don't take any more detours down lover's lane this will go a lot faster. Where is our Recreation Coordinator, Susie Rosenbaum?

SUSIE: I'm here! I'm here! I just wanted to let everyone know that the glue is *finally* dry on their pine cone and macaroni table lamps so you can come and pick them up before you leave tomorrow. *(Firmly)* And let me remind everyone *again* that you *must* take *all* of your art projects home with you. We have all of the lamps, cutting boards, and leather wallets we need up here so take them with you, please! Also, some of you haven't finished all of your projects yet, so I will be coming around to your tables to help you out. Toodles!

STUART *(hops onto the stage as* SUSIE *leaves)*: Hi, everyone. You all know me by now. I'm Stuart Evergreen, the Outdoor Education Coordinator. I think we had a great camp this year. I want to thank everyone who went on my first ever "Eat Your Way Through Nature" hike yesterday. For those of you who went, you are now well prepared to survive if you're ever lost in the woods. And based on what I saw with a few of you, that's highly likely. We ate several varieties of flowers, leaves, berries, and even some tree bark. I apologize, once again, to Mrs. Hinton. If I had know that you were allergic to fungi I would have never made you eat those wild mushrooms. I can see from here that the swelling has gone down . . . a little. Kudos to Nurse Brickman! Lastly, for anyone who's interested, I'm having a late-night skunk hunt after dinner. We're meeting down at the amphitheatre at midnight.

BIFF: I don't know about that one, Stuart. Something about it smells kind of funny. And finally we have Lester Mayfield, the world's oldest camper. As you know, Lester is our Facilities Director and has been with us since the camp started. You may not know it, but this is Lester's last summer here at camp since he has decided to retire. He is the oldest ranking member of the Bear Scouts and has earned every badge they offer. Well, every badge except one. Any progress on that one, Lester?

LESTER *(kind of down):* Nope. I still can't start a fire without matches. I've tried everything by now. I've tried it with 2 sticks. I've tried it with 2 rocks. I've tried it with a rock and a stick. I've tried it with a rock, a stick, and another rock. I've tried it with 2 sticks, a rock, and a squirrel. Boy, that one didn't go well. I've tried it with a rock, a knife, and a waffle. I've tried it with . . .

BOB *(interrupting, moving* LESTER *offstage):* That's OK, Lester. I'm sure you'll get it one of these days. Biff, why don't you help Lester out and get him something to eat? *(*BIFF *escorts* LESTER *offstage.)* Now, I just want to remind all of you folks about what we still have in store for you tonight. In addition to a delicious dinner prepared by Cookie, we have our Annual Staff Talent Show, our Camp Awards presentation, a melodrama, and lots more. I also wanted to point out that we have a competition going between our kitchen crew tonight that you get to help with. We have groups from four different camps offered here and each group is trying to win a scholarship to come to their camp for free next summer. Let's have a representative from each of those groups join me up here. *(*DEXTER, ALBERT, BUTCH, *and* ALICE *join him onstage.* BOB *says to* DEXTER *. . .)* What's your name, son?

DEXTER: I'm Dexter Applebee and I'm representing the group from the Science Camp. *(Rest of Science Camp group cheer.)* We're really hoping that good service plus speed equals a vote for Science Camp!

BOB: All right, and who's next?

BUTCH *(goes to mic):* I'm Butch McMillan and I'm here with the gang from the Sports Camp. *(Rest of Sports Camp group cheer.)* No one is going to serve you tonight faster and more competitively than we are. Vote for Sports!

BOB: OK. Remember, fast is good but so is no broken dishes. Let's see who else we have here.

ALBERT *(goes to mic):* Good evening everyone. I'm Albert Knudsen and I'm part of the Annual Band Camp. *(Rest of Band Camp group cheer.)*

BOB: Oh, I loved being in the band. What instrument do you play, Albert?

ALBERT: I'm currently the second chair triangle, but I'm hoping to move up to first this year. *(He pulls out a triangle and starts to play a song.)* That was Beethoven's 5th Symphony. Pretty good, huh?

BOB: That's, uh, great, Albert. Keep up the good work. And who is this lovely young lady here?

*(*ALICE *comes to the mic.)*

ALICE: I'm Alice Kingsbury and I represent the Loyal Order of Bonnie Belle Scouts. *(She salutes and recites their motto. If there are other Bonnie Belle girls serving they can join her.)*

A Bonnie Belle girl is honest and true
From the flower in her hat to her skirt that is blue.
We help those who suffer whether in need or poor health
And sell lots of cookies to everyone else.

BOB: Oh I just love your cookies.

ALICE: I'm glad to hear it. As a matter of fact, I'm the top seller in the state, and next month I'm going for the national title. So, how many boxes can I put you down for, Mr. Dinsdale?

BOB: Oh, uh, why don't you ask me later, dear. This isn't really the right time. *(To audience)* So, you folks will get to vote later tonight for which group you think deserves to win the scholarship. So treat our guests good tonight, kids. Before we serve dinner, let's have our camp chaplain come up and say the blessing. Let's welcome Chaplain *(Insert name of pastor or other person that will lead the blessing).*

(Pastor/Chaplain leads group in a blessing for the meal. Note: Even though this person is not a regular member of the cast, they should be instructed to dress in the style of someone from the 1940s and not to wear clothes that are contemporary. They could wear slacks, a white button-up shirt and a cardigan sweater. They also need to be instructed to speak in character with the time period and the show, and not say anything that pulls people out of the environment like, "Hey folks, how are you enjoying the show so far?")

BOB: Thank you, Chaplain. Well, enjoy your dinner everyone and we'll be back soon.

SCENE 1 BREAK

Music plays. Guests move to chow line and get their dinner (see notes on Dinner Service). Cast A circulates through the room and interacts with each table to make sure that every table gets an individual show. This will be the largest block of time that this kind of interaction with the cast will take place.

Scene 2

(BIFF enters and goes to mic. Blows on whistle to get attention. He has a box and is eating cookies out of it.)

BIFF *(while eating):* Attention everyone. We have some lost and found items as well as a few unclaimed mail packages we need to get taken care of. The first one is a box of *delicious* cookies addressed to a camper *(Insert a guest's name. Note: This guest should be a male between 18 and 35 that will be embarrassed to get a note from his mommy in front of everyone. Guest comes up to get box and BIFF finds a note inside. He reads it in a sappy voice.)* Oh, it looks like there's some kind of note in here for you, too. It says, "To my little cuppy cakes. I hope you are having the bestest happy campy time. I miss you sooooo much. I miss your itty bitty cheekie weekies and your goodnight kissy wissies. I can't wait until my little sugar booger pie comes home . . . Love Mommy." Well, *(guest's name)*, too bad you didn't get these sooner in the week. They were *very* good. (BIFF *turns over box and empties out remaining crumbs. Bell rings,* BIFF *looks around frantically.)* Where'd that come from? I gotta find that bell. *(Runs offstage)*

(BOB *and* PHOEBE DINSDALE *enter and go to the mic. They can usher the guest offstage if necessary.)*

BOB: Well, let's see how our kitchen crew competition is doing. It looks pretty even right now.

(DEXTER *comes to the stage.)*

DEXTER: Mr. Dinsdale. Some of the members of the Science Camp took the leftover tater tot grease, changed its molecular structure with baking soda, and used it to clear that clog in the septic tank.

BOB: Simply smashing work, kids. That's a point for the Science Camp. *(Science Camp group cheers.)*

PHOEBE: Bob, I think it's time we tell our guests about the changes that are coming, don't you?

BOB: Yes, I think you're right, although it breaks my heart to spoil such a wonderful evening. Ladies and gentlemen, boys and girls, as you know, Camp Awannahikealotta has been in business for almost 50 years and it's been a blessing for us to see so many people's lives changed here. Unfortunately, the camp has been losing money for the past several years—

PHOEBE *(interrupting):* More like 10 years.

BOB: Yes, well, the point is that it's been awhile now and the owners have decided to sell the camp.

(Cast members positioned around the room gasp and act surprised.)

PHOEBE: That's the bad news, but the good news, I think, is that they already have a buyer and he's here with us tonight. Will you all please welcome Mr. Franklin Abbott. *(They applaud as he enters.)* Now, Mr. Abbott has some big plans for the camp and tonight he wants to share some of them with you, our camp family, in the hopes that you'll continue to make Camp Awannahikealotta a yearly destination for you and your family. Mr. Abbott, the floor is yours.

ABBOTT: Good evening everyone. It's wonderful to see so many people who love the outdoors as much as I do. I love everything about it—the trees, the hills, the lakes, the animals. The only thing I really don't like about the outdoors is that they're, well, they're outdoors. That's why my company, CampCo, Inc., was born. Our motto is, "Bringing the Great Outdoors—Indoors." We're going to completely enclose this camp in a big plastic shell. Everything will be state of the art and you'll never again have to worry about sunburn or mosquitoes or terrifying wild life. You'll still get to enjoy everything you love about camping but from a safer, cleaner, and, most importantly, squirrel-free environment. Doesn't that sound great? *(Cast members make disapproving sounds and comments around the room.* ABBOTT *is oblivious to everyone's unhappiness with the idea.)* Anyway, I'll be talking about it more as the evening goes on. For now, I'll let you folks get back to the fun.

*(*ABBOTT *leaves.* BOB *and* PHOEBE *go to mic again.)*

PHOEBE *(forced enthusiasm):* My, doesn't that sound . . . exciting.

BOB: Now, Phoebe, nothing lasts forever. Everything changes.

PHOEBE: I know, Bob. I just can't imagine not being here anymore.

*(*STUART *and* SUSIE *rush to the stage when they hear this.)*

STUART *(anxious):* What are you saying? You're not coming back next year?

SUSIE: Please say it's not so.

BOB: Well, since the camp is being sold, we thought that it was a good time for us to retire. You know, we've been running this camp for 40 years and . . .

PHOEBE *(interrupting):* 42 years.

BOB: For 42 years and we think the time has come to let someone else take over.

STUART: Are the rest of us going to have jobs next year?

PHOEBE: That's up to Mr. Abbott, but he said that he'll need lots of help so I think he's hoping that you'll all come back.

SUSIE *(sad):* I don't know if I want to come back if you're not here. *(Hugs* MRS. DINSDALE.*)*

PHOEBE: Thanks, Susie but give him a chance and hear what he has to say before you make up your mind, OK?

STUART/SUSIE: OK.

BOB: Stuart, isn't there some unfinished business regarding some of the cabin competitions?

STUART: Oh that's right, I almost forgot. We weren't able to finish up our bird call competition this week due to the time we all had to spend tracking down the members of Cabin 7 who wandered off into the woods without a guide. It's a good thing that at least one of you had already been on my "Eat Your Way Through Nature" hike or you might have starved. So I need the best bird caller from the following tables to come up here and try and win this for your cabin. Table numbers . . . *(select four tables from your table list)*

BIRD CALL COMPETITION

Four players are selected from four different tables and are brought up onstage for the birdcall competition. They will hear a recording of an actual birdcall and then have to try and recreate it. The audience will decide who wins with their applause. *(See Individual Event Descriptions on page 63 for additional notes.)*

NURSE BRICKMAN *(enters with old fashioned flashlight; Talent Show number):* Well, everyone, it's time for that favorite part of the last evening at camp, the staff talent show. I've been selected to oversee it this year since it was learned that I have an extensive amount of entertainment experience. My several years as an usherette at the Gladys M. Showalter Performing Arts Center in Grand Rapids, Michigan, exposed me to numerous plays and musical presentations. So I've worked with the staff this year to present as professional a show as possible. First off we have a beautiful rendition of that great American song, *Yankee Doodle Dandy*. It will be played by members of our Camp Orchestra. *(ALBERT comes up behind her and says, "Ahem!".)* Oh, that's right. And featuring Mr. Albert Knudsen on the triangle.

TALENT SHOW—Camp Staff Kazoo Song

Several members of the staff and wait staff play a rendition of *Yankee Doodle Dandy* on kazoos with some singing. The more it can be broken up into different parts to sound like an orchestra, the better. ALBERT has music on a music stand. He doesn't play a note the entire song but counts along and turns the pages holding his Triangle in the air. After the very last note he hits the triangle and takes a bow. *(See Individual Event Descriptions on page 63 for additional notes.)*

*(*ANDY *and* PENNY *are playing in the orchestra and they are the last two to leave stage as* BOB *and* PHOEBE *enter and come up to the mic.)*

PHOEBE: That was beautiful, kids. Bob, did you notice Andy and Penny? They certainly make beautiful music together. *(Yelling to* ANDY *and* PENNY*)* That was wonderful you two. Keep up the great work.

BOB: Now, Phoebe. You leave those kids alone.

PHOEBE: I'm just trying to help.

BOB *(taking her offstage):* I know, but you're going to mess it up if you keep interfering . . .

(They continue to talk while walking out.)

SCENE 2 BREAK

Music plays. Servers clear tables and refill drinks.

Scene 3

BIFF *(enters and blows whistle; he has his finger wrapped in a noticeable bandage):* OK everyone, can I have your attention please? I have a couple of important things to bring to your attention. First I want to update you on our kitchen crew competition. Can I have a member of the Band Camp group come up here please? *(*ALBERT *or a different band member joins him onstage.)*

ALBERT: Yes, sir. What is it?

BIFF: I'm happy to report that the Band Camp has won a point for scaring a bear out of the camp with their rendition of the camp song.

ALBERT: That's great. *(Kind of confused)* I don't remember doing that.

BIFF: Well, it was technically an accident since the song wasn't meant to scare the bear off, but the rules allow the point anyway and I follow the rules, because rules are safety and "Safety is no accident." *(*ALBERT *says, "Safety is no accident" along with* BIFF.*)*

ALBERT: I guess a point is a point, so we'll take it. Would you like to hear us play the camp song again?

(Band Camp members crowd around excited.)

BIFF *(uncomfortable):* Uh . . . I don't think we have time for that right now, but thanks for the offer, kids.

(Band Camp members go "awww" and walk away disappointed.)

BIFF: Well, that was a close one. I have another lost and found item. *(Holds up a pair of thick, Coke-bottle glasses)* Who wants to claim them? Wow, these are thick glass. I bet you could start a fire with these.

LESTER *(calls from somewhere in the room loudly):* I'll take them! *(Comes to stage; takes glasses from* BIFF *and notices his finger.)* Biff, what happened to your finger?

BIFF *(embarrassed):* Oh, well, nothing really. I was putting up a new safety poster in the office and I hit my finger with the hammer. *(We hear the camp bell ring.)* That bell is taunting me. Excuse me, Lester. *(He runs off stage. We hear a large crash.* BIFF'S *voice calls from offstage.)* I'm OK!

*(*FRANKLIN ABBOTT *approaches* LESTER.*)*

ABBOTT: Hey, Lester. Can I talk to you for a minute?

LESTER: Sure.

ABBOTT: Wow, Lester, I'm sorry to hear that after all these years that fire-starting badge has still eluded you. I guess you could say it's your Achilles Heel.

LESTER: No, those aren't very flammable. Tried that once by rubbin' it on a rock on a hot day hoping to get a spark. *(Makes the motion with his foot)*

ABBOTT: You know, Lester, in the new camp starting a fire will be as easy as flicking a switch.

LESTER: Really?

ABBOTT: Think about it, Lester. No more wood to cut. No more laboring over kindling. No more smoke in your eyes. I have two words for you Lester—"Pro–Pane." It's the "Future of Fire," Lester. Imagine a fire pit with realistic-looking ceramic logs and fire instantaneously any time you want, with the flick of a switch.

LESTER: I don't know, Mr. Abbott. What's that going to do to the taste of the S'mores? And what about that wonderful smell of woodsy smoke that gets in your clothes and permeates the mountain air on a cold night.

ABBOTT: Well, naturally, all of that can be recreated with aerosol cans. Well, Lester, you think about it. I would love to have your help on this.

LESTER: I'll think about it. *(Beat)* What were we talking about again?

(NURSE BRICKMAN *enters wearing costume pieces over her nurse costume and goes to mic.)*

NURSE BRICKMAN: OK, you two. Scoot along. We have more important things to do than talk about fire pits. (ABBOTT *and* LESTER *exit.)* Ladies and gentlemen, boys and girls, it's time for our next talent show act. This one stars yours truly as well as Susie and Camp Counselor Esther performing a song by that famous singing trio—The Andrews Sisters. Susie and Esther, we're ready to go. (SUSIE *runs to the stage wearing costume pieces over her outfit.)* Susie, where's Esther?

SUSIE: There's good news and bad news. The bad news is that Esther is in her cabin not feeling very well. It seems that she ate a little too much tree bark on Stuart's "Eat Your Way Through Nature" hike.

STUART *(from the back of the room)*: Sorry!

NURSE BRICKMAN: Well, what are we going to do? Our number is for a trio.

SUSIE: That's the good news. I've taken care of it and found a replacement. *(Yells)* Come on out.

TALENT SHOW—Lip-Sync Number

BIFF enters very reluctantly wearing the same costume pieces and has to be pulled onto the stage by the two women. He should be wearing something bright and frilly like an apron and hat and possibly a wig. Using a song like "Chewing Gum" by the Andrews Sisters, they encourage him as the song starts and he does all of the choreography with them, but in a way that indicates that he does not want to be there. *(See Individual Event Descriptions on page 63 for more details.)*

SCENE 3 BREAK

Music Plays

Scene 4

(BIFF *enters and blows whistle to get attention. He has a bandage on the other hand this time.* COOKIE *is standing onstage.)*

BIFF: I have another update on our kitchen crew competition. Is there someone from the Bonnie Belles that can join me up here?

*(*ALICE *or a different Bonnie Belle comes to the stage.)*

ALICE: What can I do for you, Mr. Martin? Would you like to order some cookies? I still have several cases of "Nutty Buddy Choco Busters." They're two for one. How many boxes can I put you down for?

BIFF: Thank you, but I don't need any cookies.

ALICE: With all due respect, sir, everyone *needs* cookies.

BIFF: Look, I just wanted to let you know that the Bonnie Belles have won a point for creating the table decorations tonight. Congratulations. It's amazing what you can do with pinecones, glitter, and some glue.

ALICE: Why, thank you. Good job, girls. Now, I still need to know how many boxes you want to order, sir. I have quite a few boxes of Tasty Basty Butter Cookies left. And some Super Sugar Snicker Doodles, and some . . .

BIFF *(cuts her off):* Let me think about it. *(Looks out at guests and points to a table)* That guy over at Table 6 told me earlier that he really needed some cookies. Why don't you go and take his order? *(Moves her offstage.)*

COOKIE: Hey Biff, wasn't that bandage on your other hand?

BIFF: Yes, but there was a spill on the porch and I didn't want anyone to slip so I decided to clean it up. While I was mopping it up with a rag, someone walked by and stepped on my other hand with their boots.

COOKIE: Ouch. That must have hurt!

BIFF: I'm OK. Anyway, in a few minutes we're going to have our Camp Awards so be sure to stay in your seats and . . . *(bell rings offstage)* I heard that. I'm going to get that bell back if it's the last thing I do. *(Runs offstage)*

*(*ABBOTT *enters and goes to mic.)*

ABBOTT: Excuse me, folks. I thought I'd take a moment and give you some more details about the great changes you'll see at the camp next year.

COOKIE *(watching from side of stage):* I say if it ain't broke, don't fix it.

ABBOTT: But it's progress we're talking about, Cookie. Now take your kitchen, for example. You're using 30 year-old stoves and 20 year-old kitchen tools. Plus, you have to have large refrigerators to keep all of your fresh food cold. Now, in our updated and modern kitchen you won't have to worry about such trivial things as keeping food fresh. All of the food will be pre-packaged in cans and will be pre-made and pre-cooked. No more slicing, dicing, cutting, gutting or skinning.

COOKIE: But I like skinning.

ABBOTT: All you'll have to do is open a can, heat it up, and plop it on a plate. Doesn't that sound like heaven?

COOKIE: Probably not to the people eating it.

ABBOTT: You'll see. You'll have so much free time on your hands you won't know what to do with yourself.

COOKIE: That's what I'm afraid of.

(NURSE BRICKMAN *enters.)*

NURSE BRICKMAN: OK you two, that's enough shop talk for now. We have a show to do. *(Ushers them offstage)* Well, ladies and gentlemen, I'm pleased to present the next act in our staff talent show. This one involves all of you. We're going to do our annual melodrama, which, of course, I wrote and produced. Now some of you have been selected as actors and the rest of you will be following the cues for the sound effects. Won't this be exciting? Oh, and by the way, we've made some last minute changes to the storyline in light of this evening's dramatic news, so please bear with us.

MELODRAMA

The melodrama will be a story about a man taking over a family-run hotel and throwing the owners and the staff out onto the street. The storyline is based on ABBOTT taking over the camp and will be obvious to everyone in the room except ABBOTT. *(See Individual Event Descriptions on page 63 for details.)* There will be a hero, a villain [ABBOTT], a damsel in distress, a sidekick for the villain, and a dog. Members of the audience will be pulled onstage and given hats for the different characters. As the lines are read by one of the cast members, they act out the storyline. The audience will cheer and boo and make sound effects when signs are held up onstage. When it concludes, ABBOTT rushes to the stage and everyone thinks that he's going to be mad but he loves it. He obviously doesn't get that it was about him.

(As the show ends and the cast starts to leave the stage, ABBOTT *comes to the mic. He appears to be upset as he calls the actors back to the stage.)*

ABBOTT: I want to see everyone involved in this down front here right now! Come on back here everyone. That means you too. I especially want to see you! *(Once everyone is onstage he addresses them.)* I don't know what to say. That just really surprised me. The only thing I can think to say to you people is that . . . I *loved* it! I don't think I've ever seen anything quite so funny. Great job everyone! How did you ever think of that story?

(The cast looks at each other in amazement that he didn't get it. They shrug and leave the stage. ABBOTT *continues to congratulate them on the way out.* PHOEBE *enters after talent show and grabs* PENNY *and* ANDY *before they can exit.)*

PHOEBE: Not so fast you two. I was just remembering that one time I saw you two on a date at the lake and Andy was playing his guitar and serenading you while you paddled the canoe. *(*ANDY *tries to get* PHOEBE'S *attention to tell her to stop. She ignores him and keeps going.* PENNY *looks confused and frustrated.)* It was such a perfect scene with the sunset and all. You were a lucky girl back then.

PENNY *(looks angry):* I don't know who that lucky girl was but it certainly wasn't me.

ANDY *(trying to explain):* Look, Penny. That was a long time ago and it was that year that you stopped coming to camp because you moved. I didn't know if I'd ever see you again.

PENNY: I don't care. It was thoughtless of you to replace me so quickly. You should have spent an appropriate amount time being miserable and heartbroken. *(She runs off stage.)*

PHOEBE: Well, I guess I sort of threw a wrench into your reunion, Andy. I'm so sorry about that.

ANDY: It's OK, Mrs. Dinsdale. I'll figure out a way to get her back.

LESTER *(enters stage and joins them onstage):* Mrs. Dinsdale?

PHOEBE: What is it, Lester?

LESTER: It's time for something. But I forgot what it is.

PHOEBE: Well, maybe I can help you remember. Is it time for another talent number?

LESTER: No.

PHOEBE: Is it Lost and Found?

LESTER: No.

PHOEBE: An update on the Kitchen Crew competition?

LESTER: No.

PHOEBE: Is it time for dessert?

LESTER: Yeah . . . no.

PHOEBE: The only other thing I can think of is the Camp Awards.

LESTER: No. I mean yes. That's what it was. Thank you.

PHOEBE: I knew it was only a matter of time before we figured it out. Susie, are you ready with the Camp Awards Presentation?

SUSIE: I'm here Mrs. D. and ready to go. Lester, can you help me with the slide projector?

LESTER: I'll try. *(Moves to the back of the room)*

CAMP AWARDS

These awards would incorporate photos taken of guests at the beginning of the evening. Their faces would be added to pre-made slides which appear to place them in the situation at camp. They will come up and receive a certificate. *(See Individual Event Descriptions on page 63 for details.)*

- Most Improved Boater (photo of guest in canoe folded in half)
- Best Campfire Builder (photo of guest with hat on fire)
- William Tell Archery Award (photo of guest standing next to camper with an arrow through their hat)
- Achievements in Bee Keeping Award (photo of guest covered in bees with only face showing)
- Best Tree-Climber (photo of bear chasing someone up a tree)

SUSIE: Well, thank you, everyone, for another great year of memorable moments. I think everyone deserves an award, don't you? Well then, let's have some dessert!

(Cast A and B serve dessert to the audience during the break.)

SCENE 4 BREAK

Music plays

Scene 5

BIFF *(enters stage with his arm in a sling; blows whistle):* Attention Campers. I've got a few updates for you. The kitchen crew competition is heating up. Can I get someone up here from the Sports Camp? (BUTCH MCMILLAN *or a different Sports Camp member joins him onstage.)*

BUTCH: Sports Camp ready and accounted for, sir!

BIFF: Nice work, son. I'm happy to announce that the Sports Camp wins a point for clearing the tables the fastest. *(Sports Camp group cheers.)*

BUTCH: Thank you, sir! I told you that no one would clear the tables faster than the Sports Camp.

(DEXTER *joins them onstage, interrupting.)*

DEXTER: But they broke 75% of the dishes they cleared.

BIFF: I know, but I looked over the rules of this competition and nowhere does it state any penalties for breaking dishes. That's why we have rules people. Rules are safety, and "Safety is no accident."

(BUTCH *and* DEXTER *both repeat "Safety is no accident" along with* BIFF.*)*

BUTCH: After dinner we're going to wash your car really fast, Mr. Martin.

BIFF: That's not necessary, son. (BUTCH *and* DEXTER *leave stage.)*

STUART *(enters carrying a large bag or pillowcase):* Biff, what happened to your arm?

BIFF *(embarrassed):* Well, it's a funny thing. While I was restocking the first aid locker in the front office, I lost my balance and grabbed onto it and the entire thing came off the wall and fell on top of me.

STUART: Oh, that's terrible. Are you OK?

BIFF: Yes, the only real thing that was wounded was my pride. Good thing there was a sling in the locker. Speaking of pride, I want to remind the criminal mastermind behind the missing camp bell that the window for amnesty is closing fast so you better come clean. All right campers, I've got one more lost and found item. Cookie found this while she was cleaning out the meat locker. *(STUART takes out frozen boxer shorts from his bag and hands them to BIFF.)* I think I can scrape off enough of the ice to read the tag here. It says, "Property of *(insert male guest's name)*." *(Guest is encouraged to come up to the stage to take the item.)* You might want to keep better track of your stuff, Mr. *(insert male guest's name)*. I know from experience what these people are capable of. *(We hear the bell ring again.)* I'm running out of time, and limbs, to find that bell. Excuse me, Stuart.

(BIFF exits. PHOEBE enters stage carrying the bell and tries to hide it somewhere. STUART sees her and is surprised.)

STUART: Hi, Mrs. Dinsdale. Can I help you with something?

PHOEBE *(shows STUART the bell)*: Oh, Stuart. Can you help me find a place to hide this thing?

STUART *(shocked)*: Mrs. Dinsdale! You have the bell?

PHOEBE: Oh, I found it a few days ago but I realized that it was the only way to get Biff offstage and keep the evening moving so I've been using it. He'll find it soon.

STUART: He better find it before he winds up in a full body cast. Why don't you hide it out front? I think he's more likely to look for it there.

(PHOEBE leaves with the bell and ABBOTT approaches STUART.)

ABBOTT: Hey, Stuart, can I have a minute with you?

STUART: Sure, Mr. Abbott.

ABBOTT: So, I understand you're a bit of a nature boy, a real outdoorsman. *(Gives a manly punch on the shoulder)* You probably know the outdoors up here better than anyone.

STUART: I've lived off the land up here for years. Once I got lost on a hiking trip for 2 weeks. I took a wrong turn, ended up deep in the wilderness with a group from the camp. My survival skills and knowledge of the land are the reason we made it back alive. We only had to sacrifice two people for food.

ABBOTT *(kind of unnerved)*: You're kidding, right?

STUART: Oh yeah, of course. We only had to eat one.

ABBOTT *(realizing that STUART is kidding)*: You got me there, son. Good one. Well, that's exactly the sort of thing I want to talk to you about. This whole hiking outdoors thing is dangerous and it's tiring. It requires too much strain on your body and you could twist an ankle or break a leg. That's why at CampCo, we do the hiking for you!

STUART: What do you mean?

ABBOTT: Picture this, Stuart . . . your next expedition could be hike-free because we're installing . . . moving walkways.

STUART *(confused):* Moving walkways?

ABBOTT: Imagine being able to cruise through nature without having to actually lift a foot. Our wilderness walkways will navigate people through four different simulated outdoor environments and return them without any exhaustion.

STUART: You mean, take them through your *fake* outdoors. Why would anyone do that? The beauty of being outside is to experience all of the real sights and sounds of nature.

ABBOTT: We have that. Listen.

(Sound effect of nature plays. Two nature sound effects can be found on Sound Effects for Church Productions, Vol. 1 *[7-65762-05422-6] or purchased as individual MP3 downloadables at www.lillenasdrama.com).*

STUART: Well, you can't replace the smell of the great outdoors.

ABBOTT: We already have. *(Sprays aerosol in* STUART'S *face.* STUART *coughs.)* Fresh Pine scent from a can. It was developed in a government lab by biochemists. Also comes in "Skunk" and "Dew of the Morning."

STUART *(coughing):* Well, Mr. Abbott, I think that the people who come here actually like to, you know, go outside. At home they spend most of their time inside their houses and their jobs and their schools. They come up here because it's different than that and they truly enjoy getting to walk around the forest and see the trees and the plants and maybe even a deer or a squirrel.

ABBOTT *(frightened, jumps):* A squirrel? Where? Don't let it touch me!

STUART: Are you afraid of squirrels, Mr. Abbott? Is that why you want to change everything here and move it all inside?

ABBOTT: No, of course not. Not me. I, umm . . . I'm afraid of the idea of someone else getting attacked by an animal.

STUART: Someone *else* getting attacked? Were you attacked by a squirrel? It's OK, Mr. Abbott. I can help you if you want. I'm a trained outdoor educator. Tell me what happened to make you so afraid.

ABBOTT: OK. When I was little we went camping every year and I loved it. One summer when I was 9 years old, I was sitting in our camp eating some walnuts when a crazed squirrel jumped on my face and wouldn't let go until he pried the nut out of my mouth. Since then I haven't been able to get anywhere near a forest—or even a can of nuts.

STUART: Hold on just a minute. Stay here. I think I can help. (STUART *turns from the audience, reaches into a satchel he is carrying, and puts on a squirrel puppet. The puppet can also be hidden somewhere on the stage instead of in a satchel. He needs to get it on without anyone seeing him do it if possible. He turns around with it on.)* Ta-dah!

ABBOTT *(jumps and screams):* Get it away! Get it away!

STUART: It's OK, Mr. Abbott, he's not real. This is Mr. Nutters and he just wants to be your friend. *(In a funny high-pitched voice,* STUART *talks as the squirrel.)* Hi there, Mr. Abbott. Would you like to be my friend?

ABBOTT: This is ridiculous, Stuart. I'm not talking to that puppet.

STUART: You're making Mr. Nutters sad. *(Puppet hangs his head.)*

ABBOTT: No. I'm not.

STUART *(to puppet):* Are you sad, Mr. Nutters? *(Puppet shakes head up and down.)*

ABBOTT: This is silly, put that puppet away.

STUART *(as Mr. Nutters):* I'm not a puppet. I'm Mr. Nutters and I speak for all the wild animals of the forest when I say, don't be afraid of us. Except for the bears. Be very afraid of them.

ABBOTT: Oh, I will be.

STUART *(as Mr. Nutters):* We can share this great playground that God has created for us. We just have to learn to respect each other. Do you think you can respect us, Mr. Abbott?

ABBOTT: Really, come on, Stuart.

STUART *(as Mr. Nutters):* Do you?

ABBOTT *(playing along a bit now but slightly hesitant):* Yes, I can respect you.

STUART *(as Mr. Nutters):* Why don't you give me a little pat on the head to show that we're friends?

ABBOTT: OK, OK. *(He pets him.)* You know, you're really a cute little fella up close. Cutesy wootsy squirrely . . . you like a little scratch behind your ears?

STUART *(as Mr. Nutters):* OK, let's not get carried away.

ABBOTT: Thank you, Stuart. You're really helped me a lot.

STUART *(as Mr. Nutters):* What about me?

ABBOTT: Thank you too, Mr. Nutters.

*(*NURSE BRICKMAN *enters, pushes her way past* STUART *and* ABBOTT *and goes to mic.)*

NURSE BRICKMAN: OK, break it up you two. There's no room on tonight's program for your ventriloquist act, Stuart. And now, ladies and gentlemen, we come to our final performance of the evening and you're all in for a treat. The dishwashing crew will be performing their rendition of the classic ballet, "Swan Lake."

*(*ANDY *rushes to the stage and interrupts.)*

ANDY: Nurse Brickman, this is an emergency. I need to perform something right now.

NURSE BRICKMAN: But Andy, we only have room for one more number and the ballet is ready to go. I can't cancel them without a good reason.

ANDY: I need to recite a poem for Penny. It's the one I wrote for her 20 years ago. I need to show her how much I want her back. Please let me do it.

NURSE BRICKMAN: Well, I guess it's up to the folks here whether or not they'd rather see a bunch of middle-aged men in tutus performing a routine that was choreographed by yours truly or hear a poem written 20 years ago by a 15 year-old boy. What's it going to be folks, should we let Andy perform? *(Crowd, hopefully, yells its support. Either way,* NURSE BRICKMAN *finds a way to let him perform.)* OK. *(She yells to* COOKIE.*)* Cookie, can you tell the boys that they'll have to wait and do their number next year?

COOKIE *(yelling into kitchen):* Hey, ballerina boys. You can take those tutus off. You've been bumped.

TALENT SHOW—Andy's Love Poem

(See Individual Event Descriptions on page 63 for additional notes.)

ANDY: Penny. This is the poem I wrote for you when we were 15 and it says everything I want to say. I hope you like it. It's called "The Tree in My Heart."

Like a tree grows in the forest
Like a fish swims in a stream
Like a geyser attracts a tourist
Our love will always be.

Like bears love to eat honey
Like birds love to sing songs
Like flowers love when it's sunny
Our love will still be strong.

We only see each other one week a year
And when you leave I'll shed a tear
But I know our love will never depart
'Cause I carved our names
On the tree in my heart

2 good 2 be forgotten
2 hearts 2 lives 4 ever
2 good 2 be forgotten
I'll leave you never ever

We only see each other one week a year
And when you leave I'll shed a tear
But I know our love will never depart
'Cause I carved our names
On the tree in my heart

(PENNY *joins* ANDY *at some point and they finish the last two lines together.)*

ANDY: Oh, Penny. Please say that you still love me.

PENNY: I do, Andy. I'm sorry I was jealous. Do you forgive me?

ANDY: Of course I do.

(They exit hugging and talking as BOB *and* PHOEBE *come onstage.)*

PHOEBE: I knew those two were made for each other. All they needed was a little push.

BOB: Why are you so interested in them, Phoebe?

PHOEBE: Maybe because they remind me of another young couple I used to know that met at another camp oh so many years ago.

BOB: Now I understand. Whatever happened to that couple?

PHOEBE: Oh, they lived happily ever after, wouldn't you say?

BOB: I sure would. Now folks, don't go anywhere, we're not quite finished yet. *(They exit)*

SCENE 5 BREAK

Music Plays

Scene 6

*(*BIFF *enters triumphantly carrying the camp bell and rings it to get attention.)*

BIFF: I am happy to report that the beloved camp bell has been found and will be returned to its rightful place on the side of the camp headquarters. Thank you all for your help and patience as we have gone through this traumatic experience. Now I know that many of you think that pranks like freezing someone's underwear or taking the camp bell are funny, but they're not. *(As he talks,* BIFF *pats his chest and begins to notice that his whistle is gone.)* I myself have been on the receiving end of numerous pranks over the years and I don't find them the least bit funny. I think that . . . Where's my whistle? All right, who took my whistle? I give up.

*(*BIFF *leaves.* ABBOTT *goes to mic.)*

ABBOTT: I just wanted to thank all of you for making me feel so welcome here tonight. Can I have the camp staff join me up here onstage? *(The entire staff comes to the stage. The members of the kitchen crew can stand down in front of the stage if there is not room on the stage.)* Come on up, everyone. I truly hope that you'll all consider coming back next year even though things will look a little different. We'd love to have you. I wish I could talk the Dinsdales into coming back too, but I know they have their hearts set on retiring.

BOB: Yes, we do. We really want to thank you all for making our 40 years here . . .

PHOEBE *(interrupting)*: 42 years.

BOB: . . . for making our 42 years here at Camp Awannahikealotta as wonderful as they could be. Phoebe and I will treasure our memories of this place and of all of you. This meeting room is so full of memories. I can't look at these walls without seeing a story in everything here. Like this picture here. *(He takes photo off the wall.)* This is a photograph of the very first group of campers to stay here in 1896. Back then they only had tents. There were no buildings yet. They actually laid the foundations for many of the buildings we have today including this one.

*(*PHOEBE *goes to the wall and removes another photo.)*

PHOEBE: This picture shows the first person to be baptized at this camp. It was in the wintertime so you know that they were really serious about their commitment.

(Other staff begins to join in on the "show and tell." LESTER *brings up an old radio.)*

LESTER: This radio was the first one we ever had here at the camp. We got it in 1925 and it's brought us news from around the country and around the world. It was on this radio that we heard that we were going to war in 1941.

PHOEBE: And then we listened with excitement as it ended in 1945. What an amazing broadcast that was.

*(*BIFF *salutes the flag.)*

BIFF: This flag was brought here by the first group of World War 1 veterans that came here when it was used as a recovery center for them after that war. They had carried this flag with them all through their tour of duty and they wanted to leave it because they found such peace here.

*(*SUSIE *takes a painting down.)*

SUSIE: My grandmother painted this when she came here as a young girl. She loved the mountains and she especially loved this place. I'm the third generation of women in my family to come here. I'm just sad that it won't be the same for my kids in the future.

*(*ANDY *picks up a paddle that is leaning against the wall.)*

ANDY: This paddle is here to commemorate 1925, which is the only year since the camp was started that we didn't lose any boats.

*(*COOKIE *takes a rough wooden cross down.)*

COOKIE: This cross was made from some of the salvaged wood from when the kitchen burned down in the winter of 1915. People thought it was a tragedy until they realized that if the fire had happened in the summer when there were people here, it could have cost many lives. This cross was made to remind us that there are bigger things happening than we are aware of.

(NURSE BRICKMAN *takes a plaque down.)*

NURSE BRICKMAN: This is the dedication plaque that was made in 1898 by that first group of campers in the photo. My great grandfather was one of those men. He hoped that this would be a place that people could come to with their families and get refreshed by nature and learn about the God who created it all.

(STUART *removes the deer head.)*

STUART: I'd like to keep this if I could. I'm responsible for him being here.

BOB: Why Stuart, I didn't know you were a hunter.

STUART: I'm not. Several years ago when my dad was driving me to camp we hit it with our Buick.

(ABBOTT *is very moved by all of this and he steps to the mic.)*

ABBOTT: It's taken me awhile, but I've finally come to realize what this place is really about. It's not about the mountains or the trees or the lakes. It's about the people. The people that built this place and the people that they built it for. I don't want to be the guy that changes that.

PHOEBE: What are you saying, Mr. Abbott?

ABBOTT: I'm saying that I'm not going to change a thing here. I'm going to keep it exactly like it is and maintain the amazing legacy that exists here. *(Everyone cheers.)* You know, Bob and Phoebe, in order to keep this place the same I'll need the two of you to help me. Will you stay?

(BOB *and* PHOEBE *look at each and smile. They both turn and at the same time say: "Yes!" Everyone cheers.)*

BOB: Well, it looks like that wraps up another year of family camp. Have we forgotten anything?

(The wait staff yells about the contest not being finished. BIFF *steps to the mic.)*

BIFF: All right then, we need every table to make your pick for which group deserves the scholarship. Pick one of the four colored cards and hold it up. *(He counts them and announces a winner, crowd cheers. [Note: It may not be clear who actually wins so* BIFF *can select whichever group he wants to win.] After this,* ABBOTT *steps to the mic.)*

ABBOTT: You kids did such a great job I'm going to give you *all* scholarships to come back next year. *(The kids all cheer.)*

(Smoke pops out of the kitchen door/window. COOKIE *enters carrying a piece of burnt toast. [Note: If there is not a door incorporated into the set you can have* COOKIE *enter from the back of the room carrying the burnt toast. The smoke is optional.])*

COOKIE: Hey! Who left this piece of toast in the toaster? It caught on fire and stunk up my entire kitchen.

*(*LESTER *comes forward and confesses.)*

LESTER: Sorry, Cookie. I needed a snack. I put it in the toaster and forgot about it.

SUSIE: Wait a minute. Cookie, did you say that the toast caught fire?

COOKIE: Yeah. So what?

SUSIE: Don't you see. If that's true then Lester finally started a fire without matches.

COOKIE: You're right.

LESTER: I don't know what to say? Does it count?

BOB: As far as I'm concerned it does. Congratulations, Lester. You've finally earned your final Bear Badge. *(Everyone cheers.* BOB *pins on the badge.)* So what do you say, Lester. Are you willing to join us and come back next year?

LESTER: For what?

BOB: For what else? For family camp.

LESTER: I'll be there. But you better remind me.

BOB: Oh, I will. Goodnight, everybody, and thanks for another great year.

(Music plays and the cast takes their bows. They exit and lights down.)

Appendixes

Timeline

Pre-Show

- Cast A and B welcome guests and help them find their tables
- Drinks are served
- Improv with guests

Scene 1

- Bob and Phoebe Dinsdale intro
- All recite camp motto
- Biff intros camp staff
- Scene 1 Break
    - Dinner served
    - Cast improv at tables

Scene 2

- Biff—Lost & Found/Cookies, Science Camp point
- Bob and Phoebe—Bad News, Intro Abbott
- Bird Call Competition
- Talent Show—Camp Staff Kazoo Song
- Scene 2 Break

Scene 3

- Biff—Music Camp point
- Abbott and Lester—Fire pit talk
- Talent Show—Lip-Sync Song
- Scene 3 Break—Find Melodrama Actors

Scene 4

- Biff—Bonnie Belle point
- Abbott and Cookie—Kitchen talk
- Melodrama
- Andy and Penny fight
- Camp Awards with Susie
- Scene 4 Break—Dessert is served by cast

Scene 5

- Biff—Sports Camp point, Lost & Found/Boxers
- Phoebe has the bell
- Abbott, Stuart, and Mr. Nutters
- Talent Show—Andy's Love Poem
- Scene 5 Break

Scene 6

- Biff—Bell returned, whistle missing
- Staff remembers camp/Abbott changes mind
- Kitchen Crew wrap up
- Lester's burnt toast

Individual Event Descriptions

Scene 2

Bird Call Competition: This is a competition run by Stuart. The script says that they were unable to complete it during the week because members of Cabin 7 got lost in the woods and everyone had to spend time looking for them (an ongoing joke throughout the evening). The competition needs to be completed now so he calls up the best bird callers from four of the tables in the audience. He can either name names or let each table decide who to send. He speaks to them as if they know exactly how it works since, according to the script, they had been at camp and have already seen it. For example, he might say something like, "Now, of course, you all know how this works, right? We play a recording of an actual bird call and you need to repeat it as closely as possible." As it goes along he might make comments like, "I'll give you a clue. I think that one is the male" or, "Cabin 6, are you sure this is your best bird caller?" He is free to improv and joke around with the guests. Once the four calls are complete he lets the audience decide who wins by their applause. A simple trophy or certificate can be given to the winner.

Talent Show—Camp Staff Kazoo Song: This is the first of the staff Talent Show numbers during the evening. It can be performed by any number of people from Cast A and Cast B. They play a rendition of *Yankee Doodle Dandy* on kazoos that also includes some singing. The more it can be broken up into different parts to sound like an orchestra, the better. Albert, from the Music Camp, has music on a music stand. He doesn't play a note the entire song but counts along and turns the pages holding his Triangle in the air. After the very last note he hits the triangle and takes a bow.

- To the tune of *Yankee Doodle Dandy*
- To break it down, here are the parts of the actual lyric.

Verse

Yankee Doodle went to London riding on a pony
Stuck a feather in his cap and called it macaroni

Chorus

Yankee Doodle keep it up
Yankee Doodle Dandy
Mind the music and the step
And with the girls be handy

For this version we will go through the entire song 3 times.

1. The first time through the entire song is all on Kazoos.

2. The second time through it is mostly sung with a couple of lines played on the Kazoo.

Verse

Camp Awannahikealotta
Best camp in the nation
People come from everywhere
To enjoy God's Creation

Chorus

Kazoo: Da da da da da da da
The fish are always biting
Kazoo: Da da da da da da da
And campfires are igniting.

LESTER: Where?

3. The third time through the verse is instrumental and the chorus is sung.

Verse

All on Kazoos

Chorus

Camp Awannahikealotta
Gather up your camp gear
Pack it up and take it home
We'll see you all back next year!

Triangle - Ding! (Albert plays after last note is sung and takes a bow).

Scene 3

Talent Show—Lip-Sync Number: This is the second number in the Staff Talent Show and it is supposed to be performed by Nurse Brickman, Susie and Camp Counselor Esther (who is an unseen character). Esther is ill and they need a third person. Susie coerces Biff into joining them which the audience does not know until he enters dressed in the same costume pieces that Nurse Brickman and Susie are wearing. The costume pieces can include a hat, frilly apron and possibly a wig for Biff. They should be easily removable since Biff returns to the stage soon after the number.

Biff reluctantly participates and does the choreography very halfheartedly. He can either do this the entire song or he can get into it about halfway through and really start to enjoy it. Nurse Brickman should do the entire act all out and not even concern herself with Biff. She is in her own world and is thrilled to be on the stage. Susie is the one that will deal with Biff and guide him and correct him throughout the number if needed. The song should be a trio song like something from the Andrews Sisters. Use a song like "Chewing Gum."

Scene 4

Melodrama: The melodrama will be a story about a man taking over a family-run hotel and throwing the owners and the staff out onto the street. The story line is based on Abbott taking over the camp and will be obvious to everyone in the room except Abbott. There will be a hero (based on Mr. Dinsdale), a villain (based on Mr. Abbott), a damsel in distress (based on Mrs. Dinsdale), a sidekick for the villain, and a dog. Members of the audience will be pulled out during the Scene 3 break and costumed. Explain to them that as the lines are read by one of the cast members, they must act out the story line and repeat whatever their character says. The audience will cheer and boo and make sound effects when signs are held up onstage. When it concludes, Abbott rushes to the stage and everyone thinks that he's going to be mad but he *loves* it. He obviously doesn't get that it was about him.

The costume elements need to be simple hats, capes, etc, than can easily be added on top of the guests' clothes.

The Narrator can be any one of the cast members. They need to be very animated and be able to read the script with excitement and get the audience and actors to get into the story. They will need to prompt the actors to repeat their lines and get the audience to play their part by creating the sound effects and cheering and booing on cue. It's a good idea to have another cast member onstage also to help move the actors into the right places when needed.

Members of Cast A or B can be in front or on the sides of the stage with signs reading "Boo" and "Yeah" that they can hold up at the appropriate times.

Cast:

NARRATOR
PENELOPE PUREHEART—The Heroine (based on Phoebe Dinsdale)
ROB WINSDALE—The Hero (based on Bob Dinsdale)
FRED BABBOTT—The Villain (based on Franklin Abbott)
SHLEP—The Dog
THE WEASEL—The Stooge Sidekick
THE AUDIENCE

Melodrama Script

Showdown at the Happy Camper's Hotel

NARRATOR: It was a beautiful sunny day in the garden grounds of the Happy Camper Hotel. The wind was whistling, (AUDIENCE *whistles)* the birds were chirping, (AUDIENCE *chirps)* and the cows were mooing in the distance. (AUDIENCE *moos)* There may have been an elephant or two and a couple of horses nearby. (AUDIENCE *makes animal noises)*

The beautiful Penelope Pureheart was out for a walk with her faithful dog Shlep the Wonder Mutt. *(Cue card—"Yeah")* Penelope was the owner and operator of the Happy Camper Hotel. Penelope said, "Oh I just love it here at the Happy Camper Hotel, Shlep. I don't ever want to leave." *(Actor repeats these lines.)* Shlep barked in agreement and was so happy he began to run in circles and bark happiness. Penelope said, "Oh Shlep, you're the best dog ever. Would you like a treat? Sit up . . . play dead . . . roll over. Good Shleppy weppy," she said as she patted his head and scratched behind his ears.

All of sudden out of nowhere, a dark storm began to roll in. The wind howled. (AUDIENCE *howls)* And the thunder crashed. (AUDIENCE *makes thunder noise)* And somewhere in the distance, a cow mooed. (AUDIENCE *moos)* That's when they entered. The evil real estate tycoon and his stooge sidekick from ChampPro Resorts. *(Cue Card—"Boo")* "Are you Penelope Pureheart?" he asked. *(*S*IDEKICK repeats everything he says.)* Penelope answered, "Yes, and who are you, might I ask?" The evil tycoon said, "My name is Fred Babbott, owner of ChampPro Resorts and this is my partner the Weasel." *(Give time for him to repeat the dialogue.)* He continued, "Your hotel is behind in the rent and if you don't pay it, ChampPro Resorts is going to take over the Happy Camper Hotel and turn it into a state of the art resort!" *(Cue Card—"Boo")* Shlep began to growl and bark at Mr. Babbott. Penelope said, "Easy, Shlep. Mr. Babbott, I won't have the money until next week. I can't pay the rent!" Mr. Babbott said, "You must pay the rent!" Penelope said, "I can't pay the rent!" They went back and forth like this. *(They go back and forth with I can't pay the rent, you must pay the rent, etc.)* Even Shlep barked, "We can't pay the rent!" And finally, they stopped.

Mr. Babbott said, "You have to have the rent by this three o'clock or we're taking your hotel," and he stormed off. Penelope began to cry. *(Wait for* PENELOPE *to cry.)* She really cried, she was wailing. Shlep curled up at her feet and kissed her hand to console his loving owner. Penelope said, "What'll we do Shlep, our dreams are all ruined." She continued to cry. Even Shlep began to cry.

Just when it seemed there was no hope for the Happy Camper Hotel, our hero Rob Winsdale enters. *(Cue Card—"Yeah")* Rob was the maintenance man at the Happy Camper Hotel. He was strong and muscular from his years of plunging and unclogging. Go ahead and show everyone your muscles Rob. *(*ROB *does muscleman poses.)* Rob said, "Penelope, I just finished unclogging the toilet in room 14." Still crying, she thanked Rob and said through her tears. "Thank you, Rob." Rob said, "No problem, it's my duty . . . I mean it's not my duty, it's my job. Why are you crying, Miss Penelope?" Penelope said, "The evil Mr. Babbott from ChampPro is going to take the deed to the hotel if I don't pay the rent by three o'clock."

Rob asked, "Why don't you just pay the rent? Penelope answered, "I can't pay the rent." "You must pay the rent," said Rob. *(They go back and forth.)* And finally, they stopped. Penelope explained, "I can pay it next week, but he is still going to take it away." Then Penelope sobbed. Rob comforted her and said, "Miss Penelope, have no fear, your hero is here! I will take care of Mr. Babbott." *(Cue Card—"Yeah")* All of a sudden out of nowhere, the skies grew dark again, the wind howled, and the thunder crashed. (AUDIENCE *makes sound effects.)* And somewhere in the distance, a cow mooed. (AUDIENCE *moos)* It began to rain. *(Have cue card people squirt water at the cast.)* It was the evil Mr. Babbott and his stooge sidekick the Weasel with a deed to the property. *(Cue Card—"Boo")* "I'm here for the rent," said Mr. Babbott. The Weasel repeated him, "Yeah, we're here for the rent!" "I can't pay the rent," said Penelope. Mr. Babbott said, "You must pay the rent!" *(They go back and forth.)* And finally, they stopped.

Babbott said in his sinister voice, "Then the deed to the Happy Camper Hotel is mine," and then he laughed the most evil laugh ever heard by human ears. *(Wait for* BABBOTT *to laugh . . . Cue Card—"Boo")* Rob stood up to Mr. Babbott and they both held onto the deed. Rob said, "Hand it over. Nobody takes away my little Miss Penelope's dreams." *(Cue Card—"Yeah")* Penelope said, "Oh my, did you just call me your Miss Penelope?" Rob said, "Miss Penelope, I've been in love with you since the day our eyes met over the clogged drain in room 22." Penelope said, "That's the most romantic thing anyone has ever said to me."

Mr. Babbott scowled and said, "That's enough from you two lovebirds. The Happy Camper Hotel is all mine!" Then he laughed his evil laugh. "Not so fast," Rob said, and he grabbed the deed. That's when a chase ensued. Round and around they went. Mr. Babbott chasing Rob. The Weasel chasing behind Mr. Babbott, and Shlep the Wonder Mutt chasing the Weasel. Round and around they went. Then finally they stopped. Then they ran a little more and stopped for good. Our hero Rob pulled out his trusty plunger and plunged Mr. Babbott in the stomach. Mr. Babbott fell to the ground and passed out. *(Cue Card—"Yeah")* The Weasel cried, "You haven't heard the last from us," and he ran as Shlep the Wonder Mutt chased him away.

Rob looked adoringly at Penelope and said, "The Happy Camper Hotel is all yours, my little Miss Penelope." Penelope looked adoringly at Rob and said, "No Rob, it's all ours." The two were married and ran the Happy Camper Hotel for years to come and they lived happily ever after."

The End *(Cue Card—"Yeah")*

•**Camp Awards Presentation:** These awards incorporate photos taken of guests at the beginning of the evening. Their faces would be added to pre-made slides which appear to place them in the situation at camp. They will come up and receive a certificate.

The slides are in a layered Photoshop format and are designed to have a photo of a face placed in from behind. Once the image is scaled and rotated to the correct position, the artwork is flattened and converted to a jpeg file. It is then transferred into whatever software is used to project the images onto the screen.

If you are able to take the photos the night of the show, you can send someone out into the room as guests arrive and tell them that you are working on the camp yearbook and need to take their picture. Since most digital cameras look very modern you can try and disguise it as an old camera or just explain it away as some newly released Kodak camera. (Note: Don't say it is a Japanese camera since World War 2 just ended and we were at war with Japan.) Someone will need to work quickly to get the slides assembled and ready to show by Scene 3, but you have plenty of time.

If that is too difficult, you can work ahead of time and take the photos in advance if you know what night certain guests will be coming. You can even work from existing photos of them and scan them.

It is helpful to know what angle you need to take for each face to fit the slide the best. Most can be head-on, but some might work better from a slight angle. The two slides that best lend themselves to women's faces are the "Best Campfire Builder" and the "Bee Keeping" slide.

- Most improved Boater (photo of guest in canoe folded in half)
- Best Campfire Builder (photo of guest with hat on fire)
- William Tell Archery Award (photo of guest standing next to camper with an arrow through their hat)
- Achievements in Bee Keeping Award (photo of guest covered in bees with only face showing)
- Best Tree Climber (photo of bear chasing someone up a tree)

This script is a rough outline of the presentation. You can add more lines to this or just improvise with the guests as they come up to get their award. It is recommended that you get the guest up to the stage before revealing their slide. You can make up certificates with their name on it and give them one before they sit down. There is also a certificate available for download from the Lillenas Drama website—File name: "Camp Award Certificate."

SUSIE: It is my honor to hand out our annual Camp Awards to those people that excelled above and beyond at some of our activities this year.

1. Our first award tonight goes to *(insert guest's name)*. Can you come up here and join me? *(Get them onstage before the slide is shown.)* Your award is for "Most Improved Boater." I think we have a photo of you. *(Slide comes up. Say to audience.)* What is so significant about this award is that you have to remember that last year he/she lost 2 canoes. This year it was only one. So, congratulations *(insert guest's name)*.

(Keep them all onstage until the end when the lights come back up.)

2. Our next award goes to *(insert guest's name. They come to stage)*. Your award tonight is for "Best Campfire Builder." *(Slide shows with hat on fire)* Wow. It's a good thing you were close to the lake. Great job, I guess.

3. Our next award goes to *(insert guest's name. They come to stage)* This award is very controversial. You know, we're the only camp in the country that still has this competition. You are the recipient of our "William Tell Archery Award." *(Slide comes on)* Congratulations *(insert guest's name)*. Let's have a round of applause for that brave assistant too.

4. Our next award goes to *(insert guest's name. They come to stage)*. You have been selected to receive or prestigious "Achievements in Bee Keeping Award" this year. *(Slide comes up)* Did any of them sting you? How long did it take to get them off? Well, it looks like the "buzz" about you around camp was true.

5. And, finally, our last award this year goes to *(insert guest's name. They come to stage)*. Your award is for "Best Tree Climber." I think we have a picture of that one too. *(Slide comes up)* Wow. That would certainly make me climb pretty fast but a win is a win, so congratulations *(insert guest's name)*.

That wraps up our Annual Camp Awards. Since you all did such a great job this year at camp I want to give everyone a prize. Your award will be a small edible confection served to you by our staff, otherwise known as dessert.

Scene 5

•Talent Show—Andy's Love Poem: This is designed to be very corny and sappy. The poem was supposed to have been written when Andy was 15 years-old, so it is not a very sophisticated piece of art, but it means a lot to Andy and Penny.

It is best to have some sentimental music playing in the background. We recommend something like, *Peer Gynt Suite No. 1, Opus 46:1, Morning Mood.* Andy needs to perform some very over-the-top hand movements as he recites the poem.

Sample:

Like a tree grows in the forest *(Hands push up like a plant growing)*
Like a fish swims in a stream *(Hands swerve back and forth like a fish)*
Like a geyser attracts a tourist *(Hands go to eyes like a pair of binoculars)*
Our love will always be *(Hands across heart)*

Like bears love to eat honey *(Claws like a bear)*
Like birds love to sing songs *(Hands flap like a bird)*
Like flowers love when it's sunny *(Hands on side of face like petals, fingers waving)*
Our love will still be strong *(Arms up in a muscle flex)*

We only see each other one week a year
(Right hand over eyes searching)
And when you leave I'll shed a tear
(Left hand over eye searching, moves to simulate a tear falling from eye)
But I know our love will never depart *(Hands across chest)*
'Cause I carved our names on the tree in my heart
(Index fingers trace the outlines of a heart from top to bottom on the last 2 lines)

2 good *(Holds up 2 fingers on left hand)*
2 be *(Holds up 2 fingers on right hand)*
forgotten

(On "forgotten", bring left hand to right hand, drop 2 left fingers and hold up 4 fingers on right hand.)

(Repeat for 2 more lines switching starting hand)

2 hearts 2 lives 4 ever
2 good 2 be forgotten
I'll leave you never ever *(Hand across chest, shakes head)*

(During the poem, PENNY *starts to move towards the stage from the back of the room looking lovingly at* ANDY*. She eventually joins him onstage and says the last verse of the poem with him and copies his hand movements as they face each other. On the last line they touch their fingertips together and trace the outline of the heart together.)*

We only see each other one week a year
(Right hand over eyes searching)
And when you leave I'll shed a tear
(Left hand over eye searching, moves to simulate a tear falling from eye)
But I know our love will never depart *(Hands across chest)*
'Cause I carved our names on the tree in my heart
(Index fingers trace the outlines of a heart on the line)

Cast Descriptions

This show is designed to feature actors of many different ages from teenagers to senior citizens. Some younger actors can be cast to play the older characters, but it is preferable if you can find actors of the appropriate age if possible.

One of the elements of the *Family Camp* show is interacting with the guests. Since the premise is that they have been at the camp the whole week, the characters have the opportunity to really make people feel more a part of the show rather than just watching it passively. As guests are coming in, and in between scenes, is a great time for this to happen. While there are some specific things each character might say based on their role at camp, there are some that are general to the whole camp. For instance, you might ask a guest, "Did you guys have a great week at camp?" or "So, what's been your favorite thing about camp this last week?" It's great if you can get the guests to participate by getting them to answer questions instead of just performing for them.

Cast A:

Mr. and Mrs. Bob & Phoebe Dinsdale: Camp Managers

Character age range: Play as in their 60s to 80s

If you need to cast younger actors in their 40s or 50s for example, you can change the amount of time that they have run the camp from 42 years to 32 or 22 years.

Character type: A kindly old couple who are very sad to see the camp sold off to someone who wants to change it so much. They've decided to retire after more than 40 years as camp managers rather than come back next year. Phoebe has the habit of interrupting her husband and correcting him when he speaks. She should always do this to the audience, not directly to him.

Improv ideas: Since they have been at the camp for so long, the Dinsdales are naturals for walking around the room, recognizing all sorts of people, both young and old. They can comment on older people who have returned year after year to the camp and ask them how many years that they have been coming. If there are children with them they can tell "embarrassing" stories about their parents, like the time their dad lost his swimsuit in the lake or the time their mom accidentally fell into the vat of tuna salad on kitchen duty. They can ask people what they enjoyed about camp this year and what their favorite part was. As the evening progresses they can ask people what they think of Abbott's plan and if they plan to come back next year.

Mr. Franklin Abbott: Camp Owner

Character age range: At least in his 30s; can be anywhere between 30-60

Character type: He is a slick salesman type and very smooth. His intentions are good and he is genuinely clueless that what he is proposing for the camp is disliked by everyone. He honestly thinks that he is doing something that's good for them. He is not mean and controlling, just unaware.

His company, CampCo, Inc. (Motto: We Bring the Great Outdoors—Indoors!) has recently purchased the camp and has decided to modernize the entire facility and remove all of its woodsy charm. He is here to try and convince these returning guests and the staff to come back the following year to see all of his "improvements." It turns out that his desire for this comes from a traumatic experience with a squirrel when he was 9.

Improv ideas: Mr. Abbott's character would not interact with people until after he has been introduced to the camp in Scene 2. Later in the show, he might talk to people about the changes at camp. "Are you excited about the future of the camping?" After the scene with Cookie about the modern kitchen, he might talk to people about his Meal in a Can. "The top layer is an appetizer, the next sliced layer is your vegetable, the following layer is the meat entrée and the bottom is dessert . . . if you'd like, open the can on the other side and have dessert first."

Biff Martin: Camp Director

Character age range: At least in his 20s; good age would be about 30-40

Character type: A former Marine who makes it his job to remind everyone of the safety rules around camp as well as reminding them of upcoming events. Since this is the last night at camp, he is wrapping up loose ends including trying to track down "misplaced" items like the camp bell, while trying to avoid being on the receiving end of numerous pranks. Despite his constant reminder that rules are safety and "Safety is no accident," every time he shows up he seems to have another injury. Biff is stern, but he should not come off as angry. There are a couple of scenes where he gets softer or embarrassed and those are important.

Improv ideas: Biff could interrogate people about the missing bell. He might also ask people their name and see if they are on his list of those who owe money to the snack shack. He also might remind them of the rules at camp. He can also tell stories to kids about some of the pranks that their parents pulled when they were little.

Lester Goodson: The "World's Oldest Camper"

Character age range: Since Lester has been with the camp since it started 50 years ago, he should at least be in his 70s. You can get someone in their 40s or 50s and age them to play Lester or find someone the right age to play him.

Character type: He is a funny character and needs a strong actor to bring out the humor. Lester has been with the camp since it started and has climbed the promotions ladder as high as he can go. Unfortunately, he can't make that last rung because of his inability to complete the one camp task required to be promoted to this level—starting a fire without matches. Lester also has a tendency to be a little forgetful, which might actually come in handy this evening.

Improv ideas: Lester might ask people tips on how to start a fire. He could even try to use items that belong to people to try. He might reminisce about the old days at camp when they slept in tents with holes in them and had to kill and cook their own meals.

Nurse Brickman: Camp Nurse

Character age range: She can be any age but should not be younger than 25 or so since she does talk about her several years of theatre experiences as well as her nursing training.

Character type: She is the "nurse with a heart." She will be on call all evening to finish bandaging those cuts, scrapes, and poison ivy outbreaks. She also runs the staff talent show due to her extensive entertainment experience that came from being an usher for several years.

Improv ideas: She could assume people have been to see her earlier in the week for various ailments and ask how they are recovering. Be careful not to say anything too embarrassing. She could diagnose someone with a problem and administer bandages. She might also discuss her extensive theatre background with guests and ask them how they enjoyed her performance.

Cookie: Camp "Chef"

Character age range: Cookie could be anywhere from 35-60

Character type: A colorful and slightly gruff female or male character who doesn't shy away from using "locally acquired" meat in some of his/her creations like his/her famous "Squirrel Stew." He/She is also a master at acquiring any World War 2 surplus food items to stretch the camp's food budget.

Improv ideas: Cookie can discuss tonight's food with the guests and get their input. If you decide to tell people it is something like squirrel, she can ask them if they've ever had it before and let them know that she trapped everything herself. Discuss all the local game meats and share recipes on how to cook them.

Susie Rosenbaum: Recreation Coordinator

Character age range: Play as in her 20s or early 30s

Character type: She is young and spunky and enthusiastic about life. A spunky girl who is making sure that everyone finishes their craft projects before the evening is over.

Improv ideas: Being the recreation and crafts coordinator, she should walk around to the tables and have people finish their crafts like leather wallets. These can be purchased online and started before being given to the guests to finish. She could talk to them about the beautiful macaroni lampshades people made and remind people to take them home. She could talk about other crafts made with ridiculous items. She might have a tool belt with tape, glue, etc, that she can use to help guests finish their projects or repair their personal belongings.

Stuart Evergreen: Outdoor Education Coordinator

Character age range: Plays as in his 20s, but can also be older—40s or 50s

Character type: He is a "career camper." An earthy nature boy, Stuart can't help but share his vast knowledge of all things outdoors including the various kinds of local plants that are edible. He is kind of a nerdy but lovable boy scout. He uses his puppet therapy skills to help Mr. Abbott overcome his fear of wildlife. Note: We recommend not revealing the "Mr. Nutters" puppet until he shows up in Scene 5. While it would be a funny prop to use with the guests, it spoils the joke for later in the show. After Scene 5 he can share it with the guests.

Improv ideas: Stuart can talk to people who may have gone on his "Eat Your Way Through Nature" hike and ask them what their favorite thing to eat was. He might talk about different kinds of Jerky . . . "squirrel, rabbit, owl, etc.," and could even play a round of "Name That Jerky" with some guests. He might also tell stories of surviving in the woods.

Andy Thompson: Aquatic Director

Character age range: Andy's and Penny's ages should be roughly the same. The reference to the poem written 20 years ago (when they were 15) works if they are 35 years old in the show. If you cast younger (or older) actors, you need to adjust the age of the poem to fit. For example, if Andy and Penny are played by 25 year-olds, then the poem would have been written 10 years ago when they were 15. There are other age and time references in the script that have to do with these two characters that would also need to be adjusted.

Character type: Andy has been working here for 10 years but came to this camp when he was a boy. What makes this year special is that his camp romance from 20 years ago has returned with her brother's family for the week. She has never married and the two of them have been getting to know each other again. At the end of the evening, Andy recites a poem to her that he wrote when they were 15. It's pretty bad, but she joins him in a love-struck duet at the end of it.

Improv ideas: Andy could talk to people about which activities they did this week. He could ask people why they didn't show up for the polar bear swim. He might talk to people about sinking their canoe, losing paddles, and his relationship with Penny. He can joke with some of the guys about their inability to swim out to the raft. He can encourage them and tell them that he's sure that they will make it next year.

Penny Knight: Andy's former camp romance

Character age range: See note above about Andy's age

Character type: She's carried a torch for Andy, but she's not sure if they're right for each other until Andy recites the poem he wrote for her when they were 15 years old.

Improv ideas: Penny will mostly talk about her camp romance with Andy. She can go to different tables and introduce Andy to her "family." She can do this at several different tables since they won't be able to hear what happens elsewhere. After they have their falling out, she can ask people for advice. Even though she is not camp staff, she can participate in some of the activities that place her on the stage with Andy at the right time.

Cast B (Kitchen Crew):

This group is composed of four smaller groups of people representing four upcoming camps: Science Camp, Sports Camp, Music Camp, and Bonnie Belles Camp. This group is designed to feature high school or college age actors. They are in a contest to see which group wins a scholarship to come to camp next summer. The guests will vote on them at the end of the evening. This group can be as small as four people or as large as you want it. There is one speaking part from each group that interacts with Cast A, but you can split that part up among different people if you want to give more people some lines. The Bonnie Belles are an all-girls group, but the other groups can be mixed. The names of the characters with speaking parts can be changed and given to girls. They do not need to be males.

These groups are the crew that come in and bus the tables, refill drinks, and serve dessert to the guests. They can interact and improv with the guests if they are capable of it, but are not required to. That is mostly done by Cast A. Each group is trying to win votes so they should be talking with the guests enough to try and win their vote. Each group should be identified by a color that matches a colored card on each table that the guests will use to vote with. The camp logo can be printed on four different color shirts that they can wear or you could use four different colored bandanas. Each group would personalize their costume based on their type of camp.

Dexter/Dina Applebee: Science Camp Team Leader

Character type: He/She is kind of nerdy and likes to do experiments with condiments and table items. The actors in this group might wear lab coats over their costumes, thick glasses, high water pants, etc. This group can have both men and women.

Improv ideas: He/She's trying to earn points for science camp so he/she might do experiments with items at the tables.

Albert/Alison Knudsen

Character type: Is currently second triangle in his/her school's orchestra but is trying to be first. He/She practices with the help of the guests. The members of this group should wear something casual like jeans for the boys and skirts for the girls. They could carry other instruments around or even wear marching band hats. This group can have both men and women.

Improv ideas: He/She can perform triangle symphonies for the guests and can also give triangle lessons, letting people try too.

Butch/Betty McMillan: Local High School Track Star

Character type: Prides himself/herself on how fast he/she can clean a table off. This group should wear something casual like jeans for the boys and skirts for the girls, and can embellish them with sports caps, sweaters, jerseys or letterman jackets. Be careful of anything that has a year on it that is contemporary. This group can have both men and women.

Improv ideas: Butch/Betty can brag about his/her various sports accomplishments. Show his/her badges and trophies. Maybe show how many pushups he/she can do or bicep curls with table items.

Alice Kingsbury

Character type: Top cookie seller in the state and is going for the national title. She takes cookie orders from the guests at her tables and recites the Bonnie Belle Pledge. It would be good to come up with some kind of simple uniform for this group like a plain circle skirt, white shirt or blouse, and a beret with a big flower on it. You can also make sashes that have badges on them. This group should be all women.

Improv ideas: Alice will try to sell, sell, sell cookies to the guests. She can teach people the Bonnie Belle Pledge and try and recruit new members.

PERFORMANCE LICENSING AGREEMENT

Lillenas Publishing Resources
Performance Licensing
P.O. Box 843336, Kansas City, MO 64141

Name ____

Organization ____

Address ____

City ___________________________ State ____ Zip __________

Play title: ***Family Camp*** by Dave Avanzino & Craig Wilson

Number of performances intended ___________________________

Approximate dates _____________________________________

Amount remitted $_____________

Mail to Lillenas at the address above.

This is a royalty play. Permission to perform this work is granted when a Production Pack is purchased and the royalty is paid two weeks prior to the performance. Order your Production Pack (7-65762-16930-2) for this script from your local bookstore or directly from the publisher 1-800-877-0700.

ROYALTY: $35.00 for the first performance; $25.00 for each subsequent performance. Payable U.S. funds.

Please feel free to photocopy this page.
GL #450-100-390